wingcanfly

Costa Rica: Unleash Freedom in the Wilderness

Travel Journal

Terence Lui

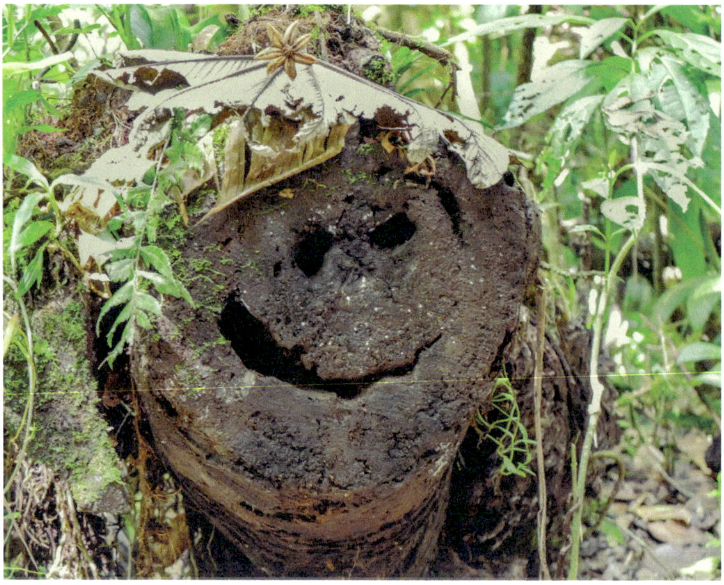

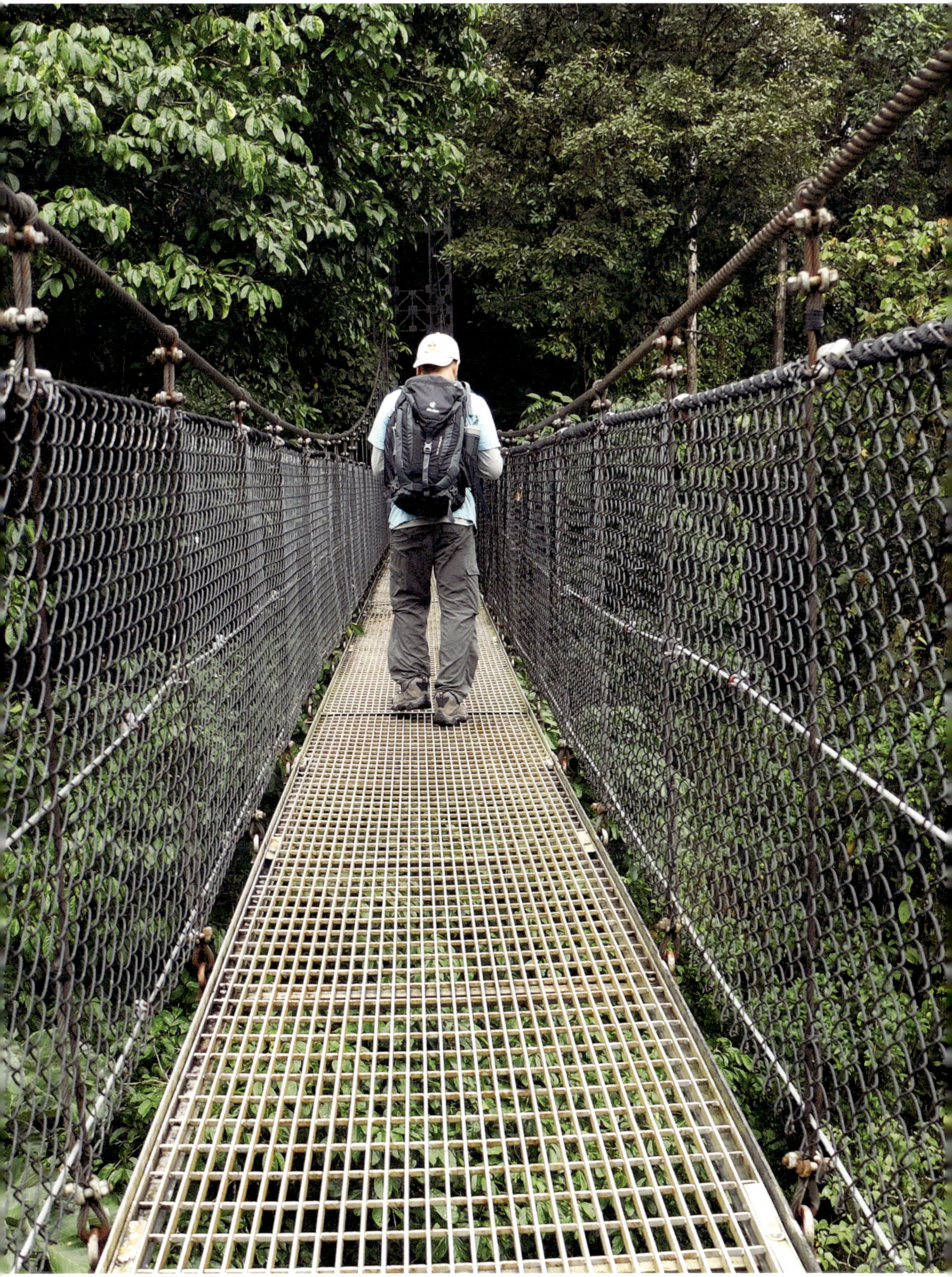

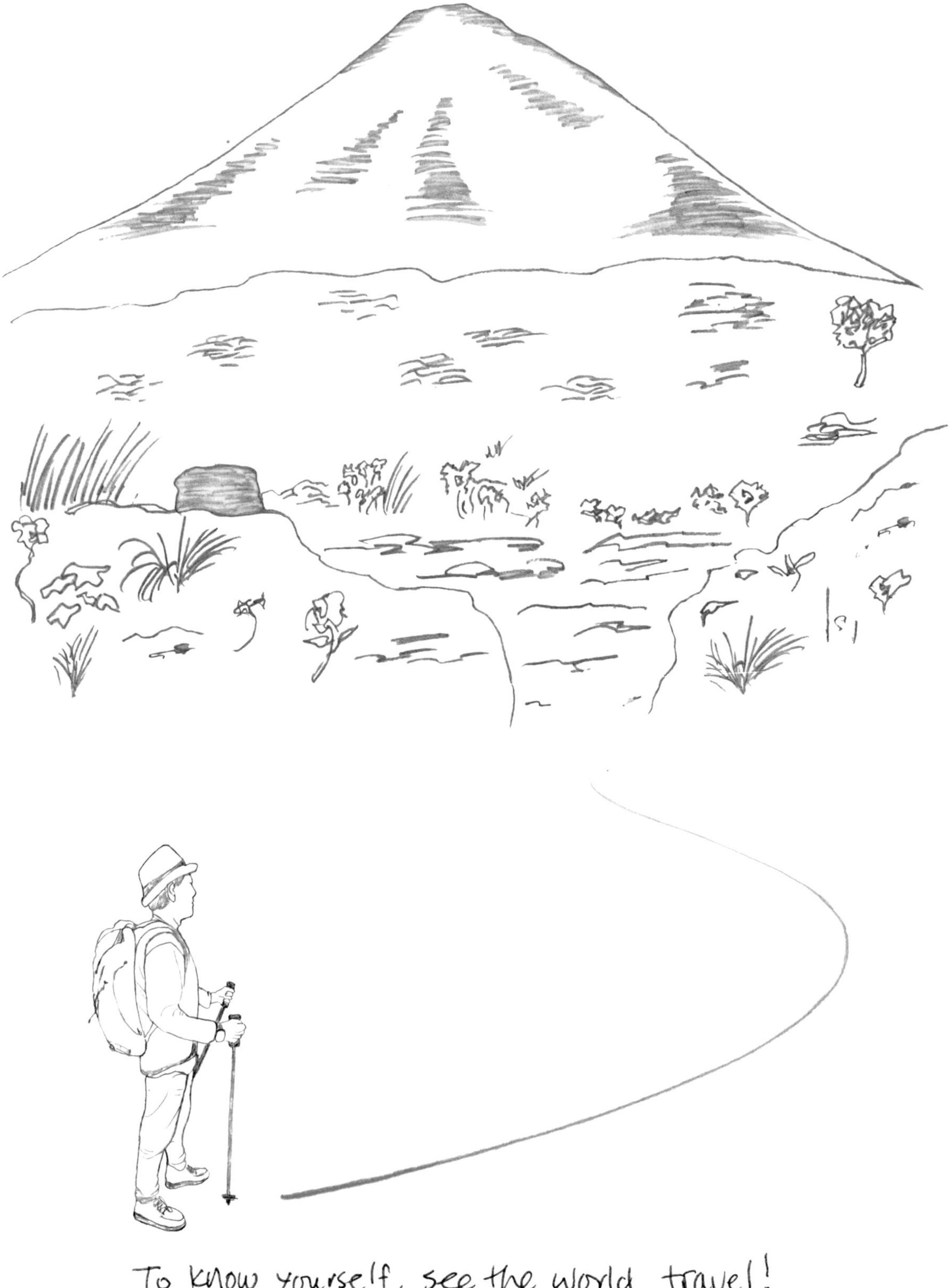

To know yourself, see the world, travel!

Introduction:
Travel and Embrace

Back in the day, I was more of a homebody – didn't really venture beyond the neighborhood. Fast forward to post-college life, and bam! I found myself solo tripping through a bunch of European cities with just a backpack on my back. Three weeks of pure wanderlust, and it blew my mind.

Now, I wasn't out there for ages, but those three weeks were like a crash course in humanity's rich tapestry. People, lives, and cultures, all hiding out in the nooks and crannies of this big ol' world. And let me tell you, it got me hooked on this whole exploration thing.

So, someone once asked me, "Why bother planning your own trips? Just hop on a tour and let them do the heavy lifting." Well, my friend, doing your homework before traveling is like getting a sneak peek into a destination's heart and soul. You pick up on its rhythms, quirks, and hidden gems, enriching your experience. Also, understanding its history adds another layer of appreciation to your journey. And most importantly, it's all about that sweet, sweet freedom.

Being the captain of my own ship, so to speak, gives me a thrill like no other. There's a sense of empowerment in knowing that I get to decide where to go, what to see, and how to make the most of my time in a new place.

Sure, I've had a buddy or two tag along occasionally, just like on this Costa Rica trip. But solo travel is my jam. Why? Because being the master of my own itinerary means I can change plans on a whim, wander into random places, and soak up the thrill of spontaneous adventure. There's nothing quite like bumping into a fellow explorer mid-journey, sharing a killer view, snapping pics separately, bonding over coffee, swapping emails, and then waving goodbye, not knowing if our paths will ever cross again. It's a wild ride, and I'm all in for the unpredictability.

You know, besides the awesome connections you make with fellow travelers, chatting up locals adds a whole new level of fun to the journey. That's why I make it a point to hit up the local market whenever I'm on the road. There's something magical about seeing all that fresh produce and chatting with the folks who know the area best. If I'm lucky, I might even score an invite into someone's home for a homemade meal and a taste of their homemade wine – talk about a cherry on top!

And hey, if I can fit it in, I try volunteering while I'm at it. Spending a few days giving back to the community not only feels good but also helps me get to know the local culture and lifestyle. These little moments make each trip stick with me long after I've packed my bags.

Whether I'm traveling solo or with friends, my camera is always with me. Though I'm no pro photographer, snapping pics helps me capture the awesome people and places I encounter. And allow me to share with you, flipping through those photos later is like a trip down memory lane, inspiring me to jot down these adventures in my travel journal!

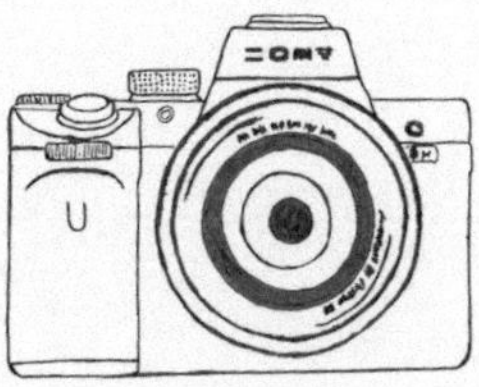

The Spanish in the Americas

Spanish exploration

1501
Rodrigo de Bastidas - A Spanish conquistador who initially explored Panama.

1502
Christopher Columbus - Ventured along the shores of Central America during his fourth expedition, bestowing upon it the name Costa Rica (Rich Coast).

Spanish conquest

1521
Hernán Cortés - Spanish conquistadors successfully subdued the Aztec Empire and its capital, resulting in Mexico becoming the Spanish colony known as New Spain.

1524-1527
Pedro de Alvarado - The Spanish conquest of Guatemala.

1540
Costa Rica is part of New Spain.

Timeline: Central

Independence

1800
Brazil was the first to gain independence from Spain.

1821
Mexico gained independence from Spain.

Costa Rica and other Central American provinces gained independence from Spain and briefly joined the Mexican Empire under Emperor Agustín de Iturbide.

1823
Guatemala declared its independence.

Guatemala, El Salvador, Honduras, Nicaragua, and Costa Rica united to form the United Provinces of Central America.

1838
The United Provinces of Central America disintegrate into individual nations due to internal conflicts and regional differences.

Costa Rica declared itself a fully sovereign nation, with Juan Mora Fernández becoming its inaugural head of state.

Costa Rica

1824
Slavery's end spans all of Costa Rica.

1828
Nicoya became part of Costa Rica and is now in the Guanacaste Province.

1848
José María Castro Madriz assumed the presidency of the Republic of Costa Rica during the period from 1848 to 1849.

16th-century Spanish conquest routes through the Caribbean, Mexico, and Central America.

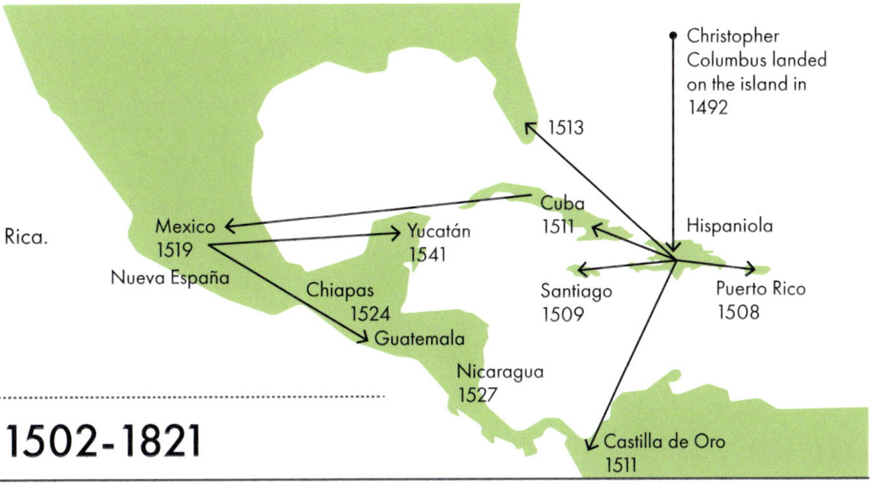

Juan de Cavallón - Led the first successful colonization of Costa Rica.

1561

Colonial Era 1502-1821

America 1501 – 1987

The death penalty was abolished during the tenure of General Tomas Guardia.

1882

San Jose was the inaugural Latin American and third global city to enjoy electric lighting.

1884

Congress annulling Otilio Ulate Blanco's election victory over Rafael Calderón Guardia triggered a six-week Civil War for the disputed presidency.

Costa Rica's army was disbanded by President Figueres Ferrer on Dec 1, 1948, after winning the civil war, resulting in enduring peace.

1948

The new constitution granted voting rights to women and people of African descent, replaced the military with a civil guard, and elected José Figueres Ferrer, a PLN co-founder, as president. His agenda included social security and bank nationalization.

1949

President Óscar Arias Sánchez won the Nobel Peace Prize for his peace plan, signed by leaders of Nicaragua, El Salvador, Guatemala, and Honduras.

1987

We seek in Central America not peace alone, not peace to be followed someday by political progress, but peace and democracy, together, indivisible, an end to the shedding of human blood, which is inseparable from an end to the suppression of human rights.

~ Óscar Arias Sánchez

Óscar Arias Sánchez served as the President of Costa Rica twice, first from 1986 to 1990, and then from 2006 to 2010. He won the Nobel Peace Prize in 1987 for his idea known as the "Arias Plan," which aimed to settle the conflict in Central America.

Costa Rica:
A Central American Oasis of Tranquility

So, imagine this sprawling patchwork quilt of land, stretching over 500,000 square kilometers, tying together seven vibrant nations like a string of pearls between the Pacific Ocean and the enchanting Caribbean Sea. Central America, they call it. But within this tapestry of diversity, there's a whole spectrum of stories.

Take a look at El Salvador, for example. It's been facing some tough stuff—like drug problems, human trafficking, and all that violence. But then, there's the Panama Canal, this amazing feat of human smarts cutting through the land, showing what we can do when we really try. And right in the middle of all that, there's Costa Rica, this beautiful place with its green jungles and tons of animals running around.

Let's rewind the clock a bit and peek into Central America's history. Once upon a time, it was the Spanish playground, until the locals said, "Nah, we're doing our own thing." Cue the birth of the United Provinces of Central America. But like most tales, unity was a fleeting affair, and soon, each slice of land decided to go its own way, paving the path to nationhood. But hey, newfound freedom didn't exactly bring peace and rainbows. Nope, there were power struggles, coups, and good ol' civil wars.

Now, let's zoom in on Costa Rica. In 1948, it was smack dab in the middle of a 44-day civil showdown, claiming lives and leaving scars. But then, something extraordinary happened. The president at the time dropped a bombshell—no more military. That's right, Costa Rica became the world's first nation to give war the boot. Fast forward to '87, and President Óscar Arias whips out the "Arias Plan," a ray of hope in troubled times. It was like music to the ears of five nations, leading to the signing of the Central American Peace Accords. And guess what? Arias even snagged himself a Nobel Peace Prize for his troubles. Talk about a game-changer.

Costa Rica—a tranquil haven where the sounds of nature trump the roar of war machines. It's like stumbling upon a quiet fishing village, cradled by the Pacific, basking in the sweet embrace of peace. And those rainforests? They're not just pretty—they're like Mother Nature's fortress, sheltering all sorts of critters and doing their bit to keep global warming at bay.

So there you have it—Costa Rica in all its glory. A little slice of paradise in the heart of Central America, where peace isn't just a dream but a way of life.

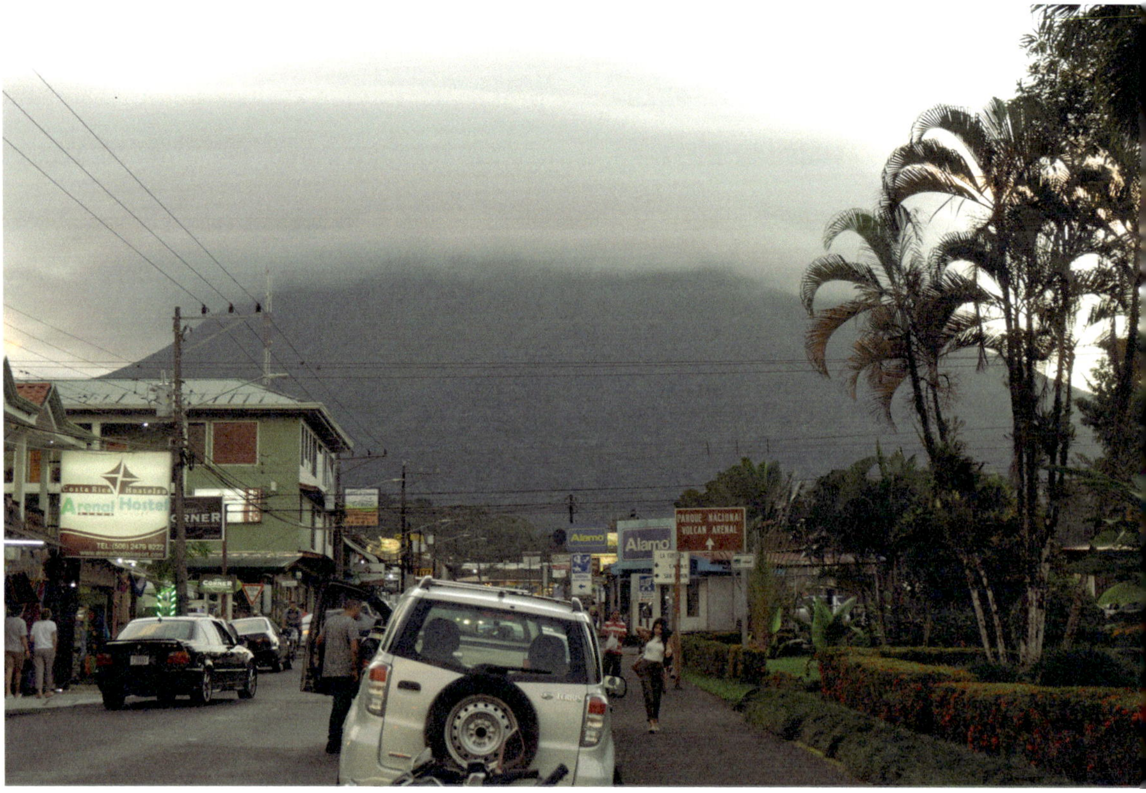

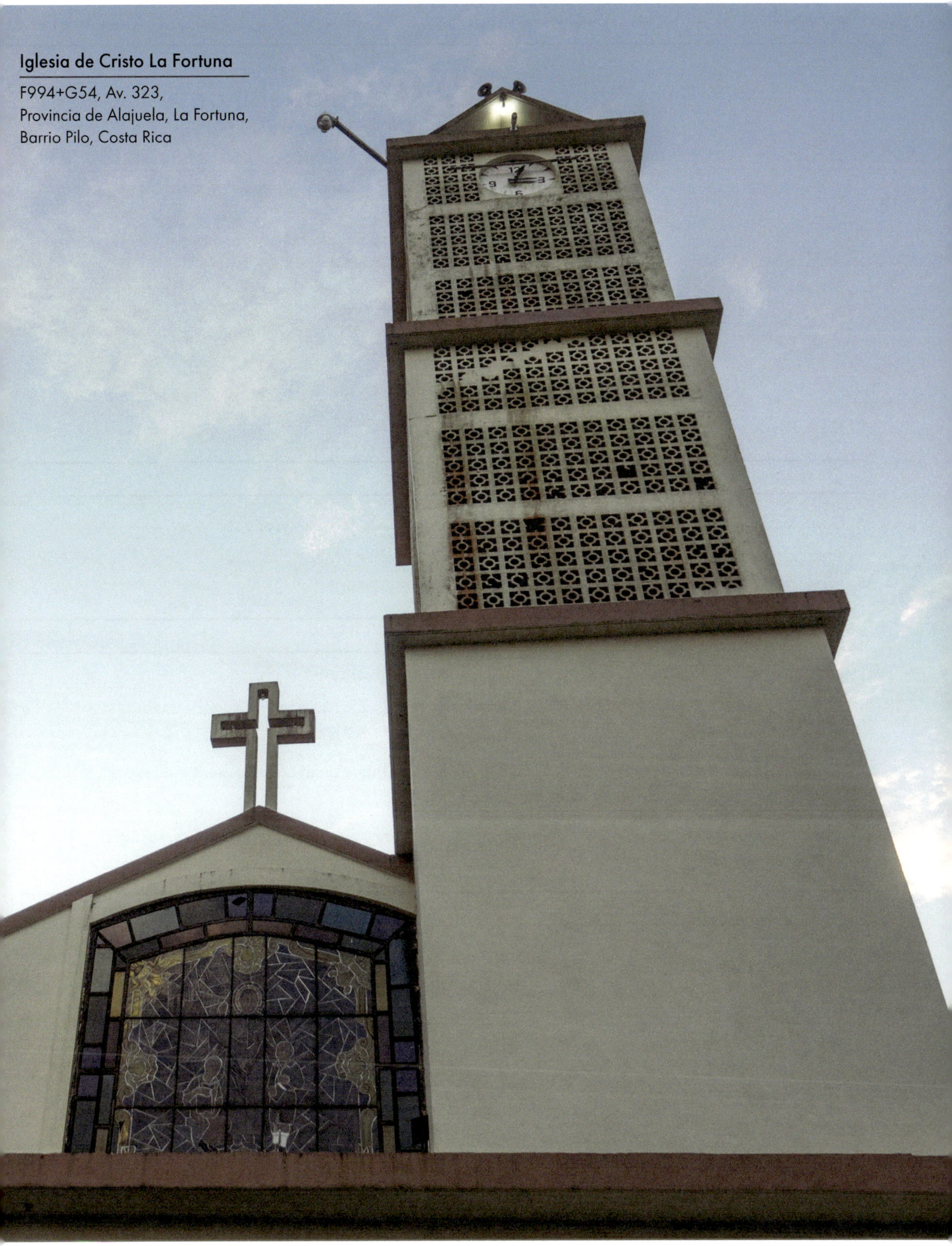

Iglesia de Cristo La Fortuna

F994+G54, Av. 323,
Provincia de Alajuela, La Fortuna,
Barrio Pilo, Costa Rica

Costa Rica facts

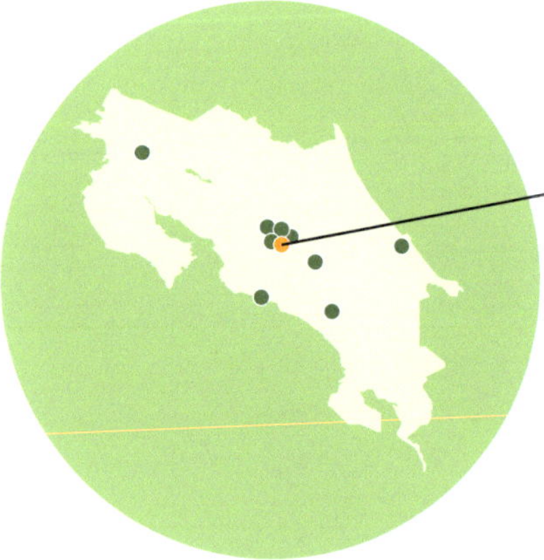

Costa Rica Population: 5.21M (2023)

- San Jose is the capital and largest city, boasting a population of 333,980 and a substantial population density of 6,455 people per square kilometer (16,720/square mile).
- The greater metropolitan area of San Jose is home to 2.15 million residents, accounting for one-third of the entire country's population.
- Costa Rica has 83.8% of its population residing in a city or the surrounding metro areas.

Overview

Costa Rica Population Rank 2023	124	Capital	San José
Area (km^2)	51,100	GDP (IMF)	$62.38
2024 Growth Rate	0.63%	GDP (UN)	$58.85 Bn

Demographics

- In the 2011 census, Costa Rica's ethnic composition included :
  66% White/Castizo, 14% Mestizo, 9% immigrants, 7% Mulatto,
  2.5% Amerindian, 1% Black, 0.2% Asian, 0.9% other
- A genome project found that individuals in the Central Valley have an average genetic makeup of 68% European, 29% Amerindian, and 3% African.
- Costa Rica houses around 104,000 indigenous people, mainly in reservations, belonging to eight distinct ethnic groups: Quitirrisi, Matambu, Maleku, Bribri, Cabécar, Guaymi, Boruca, and Térraba.

City	Population
San José	335,007
Limón	63,081
San Francisco	55,923
Alajuela	47,494
Liberia	45,380
Paraíso	39,702
Puntarenas	35,650
San Isidro	34,877
Curridabat	34,586
San Vicente	34,447

Pura Vida: Pure and Simple Living

Costa Ricans, known as 'ticos,' often use the expression 'pura vida' to convey gratitude, joy, and appreciation for a well-lived life. This versatile phrase reflects the overall happiness of Costa Rica, one of the world's happiest countries, serving as a cultural touchstone that embodies the nation's positive, vibrant spirit and deep satisfaction with life's simple joys.

Average Life Expectancy (2023)

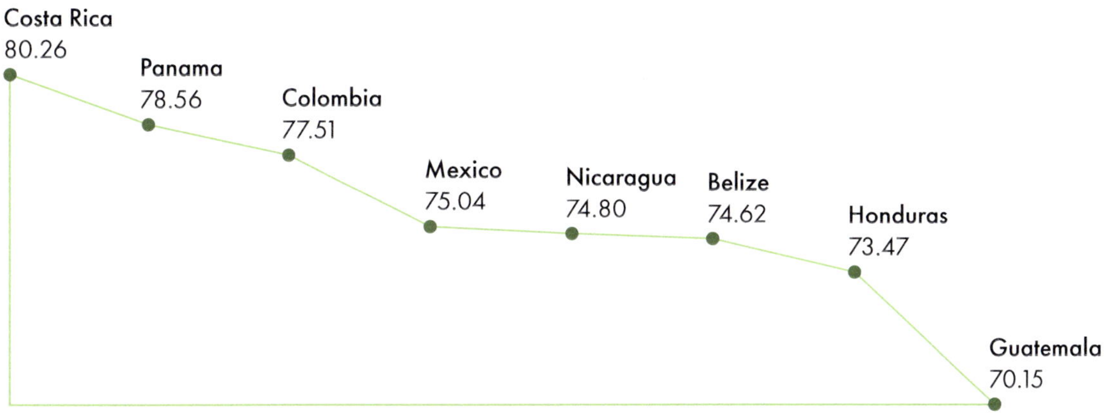

Tourism in Central and South America (2019)

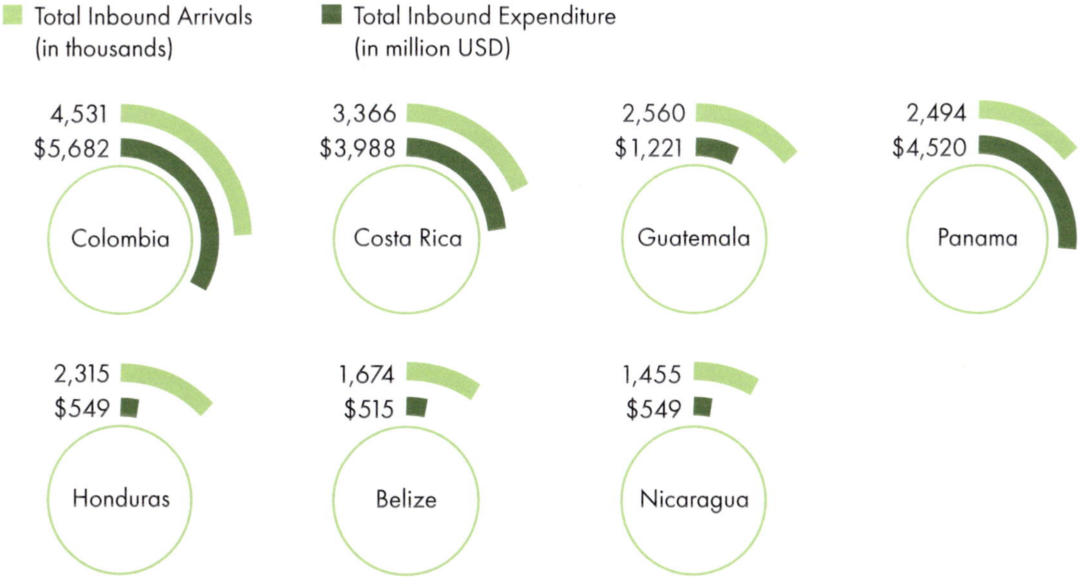

https://www.worldometers.info/world-population/costa-rica-population/
https://www.worldometers.info/demographics/life-expectancy/#countries-ranked-by-life-expectancy
https://www.unwto.org/tourism-statistics/key-tourism-statistics

The route

The journey begins at SJO International Airport, heading west to Playas del Coco by the seaside, then circling back to La Fortuna. Afterward, there's a one-day trip north to Caño Negro, completing the entire twelve-day adventure. All the photos in this journal were captured along this route.

- Juan Santamaria International Airport (SJO)
- La Fortuna
- Monteverde
- Llanos de Cortes
- Playas del Coco
- Caño Negro

International Airport

San Jose
Juan Santamaria International Airport (SJO)

Liberia
Daniel Oduber International Airport (LIR)

National Park

1. Parque Nacional Santa Rosa
2. Parque Nacional Guanacaste
3. Estación Experimental Forestal Horizontes
4. Parque Nacional Rincón de la Vieja
5. Refugio de Vida Silvestre Caño Negro
6. Parque Nacional Volcán Tenorio
7. Parque Nacional Palo Verde
8. Dr. Rafael Lucas Rodríguez Caballero Wildlife Refuge
9. Parque Nacional Volcán Arenal
10. Children's Eternal Rainforest
11. Parque Nacional Juan Castro Blanco
12. Parque Nacional Volcán Poás
13. Braulio Carrillo National Park
14. Reserva Natural Cabo Blanco

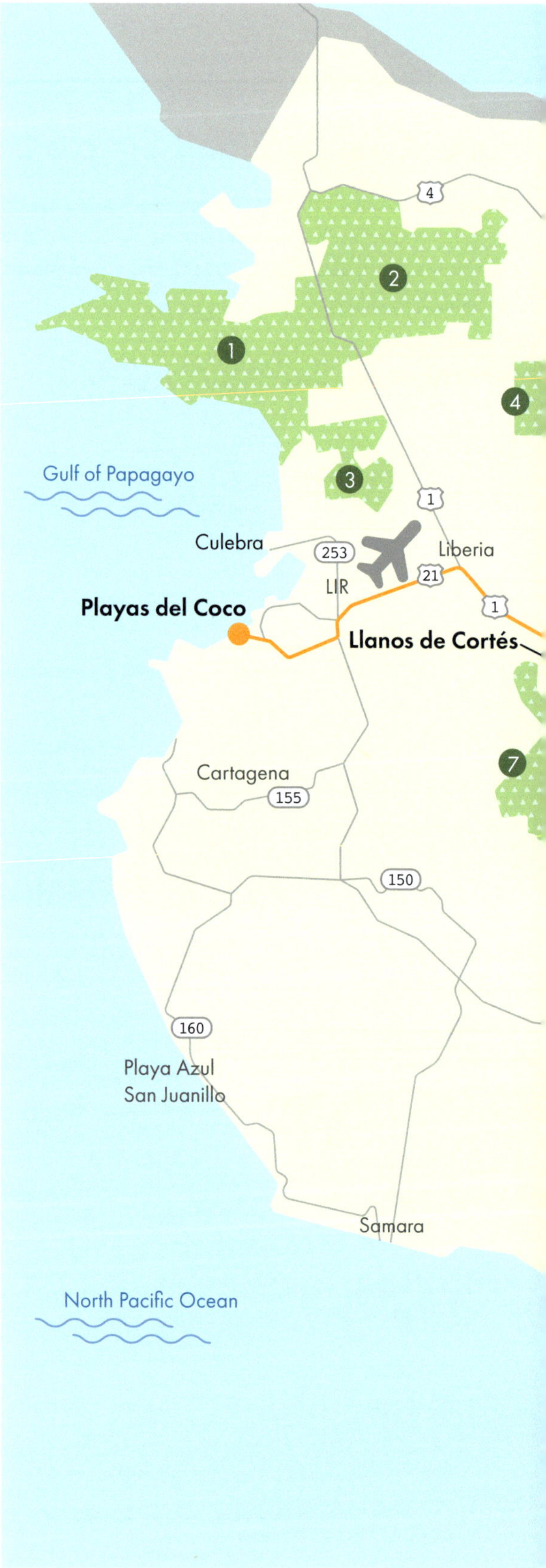

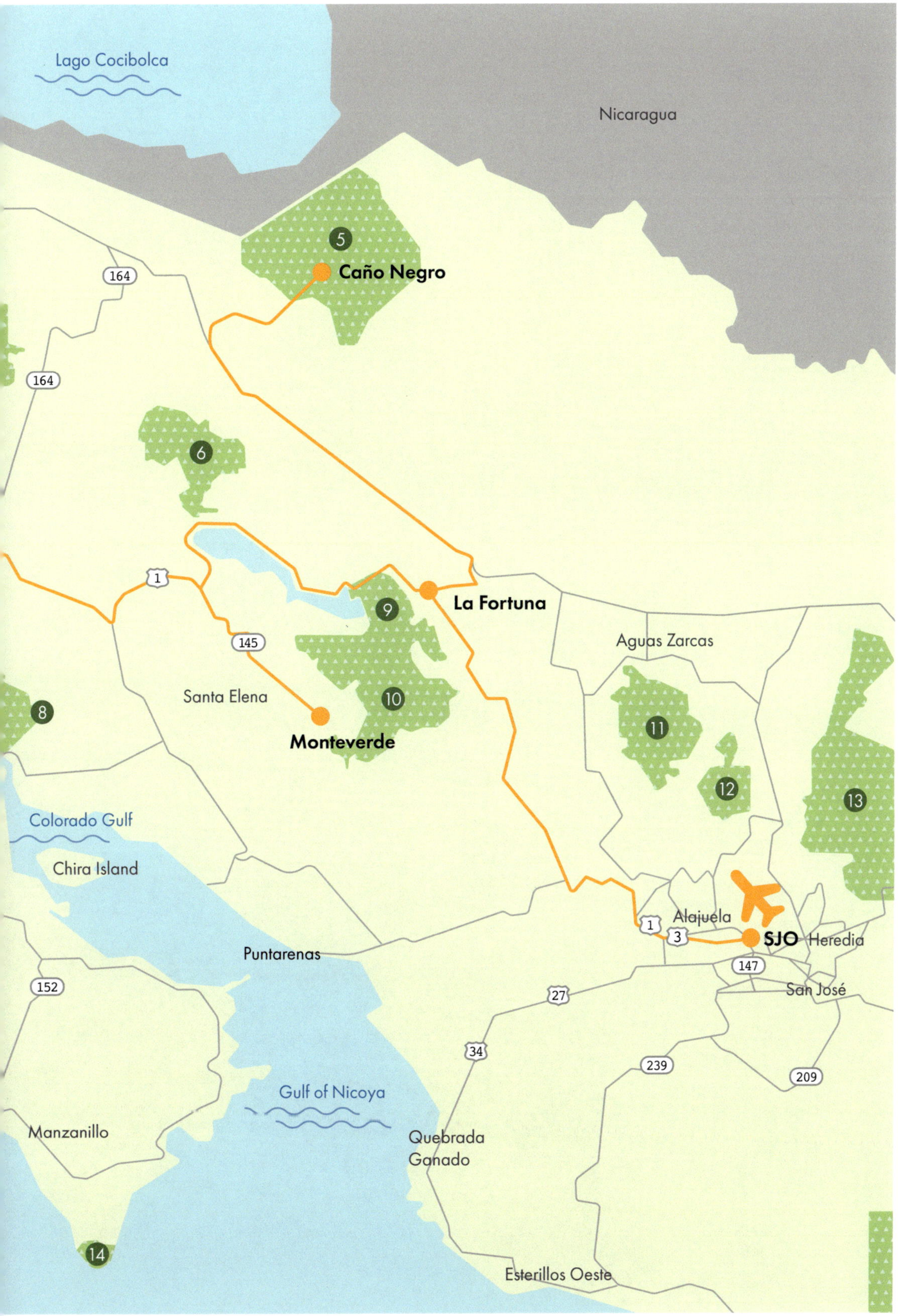
Lago Cocibolca
Nicaragua
5
Caño Negro
164
164
6
1
145
9
La Fortuna
Aguas Zarcas
Santa Elena
10
8
Monteverde
11
12
13
Colorado Gulf
Chira Island
1
Alajuela
3
SJO
Heredia
147
San José
Puntarenas
152
27
34
239
209
Gulf of Nicoya
Manzanillo
Quebrada
Ganado
14
Esterillos Oeste

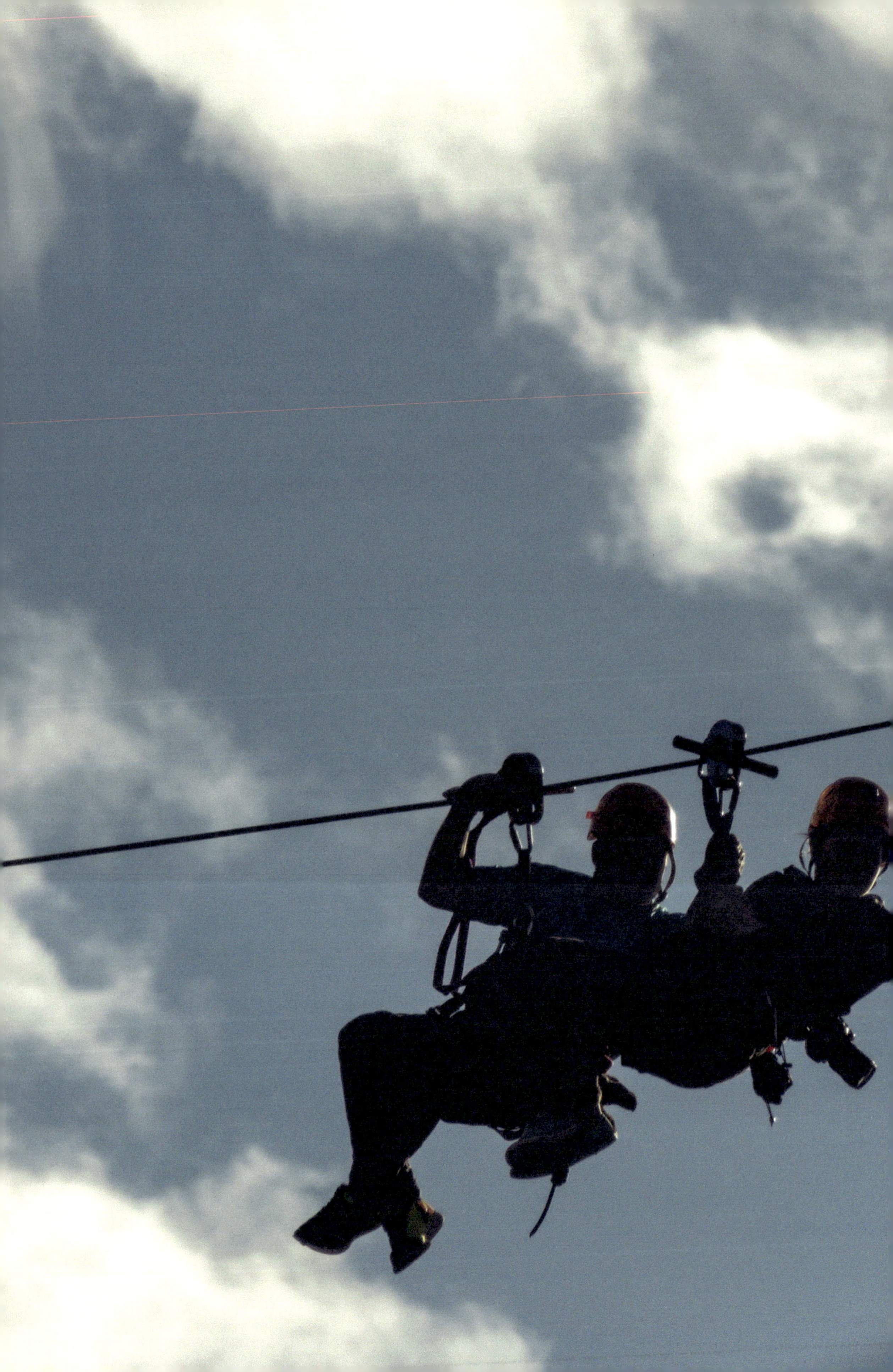

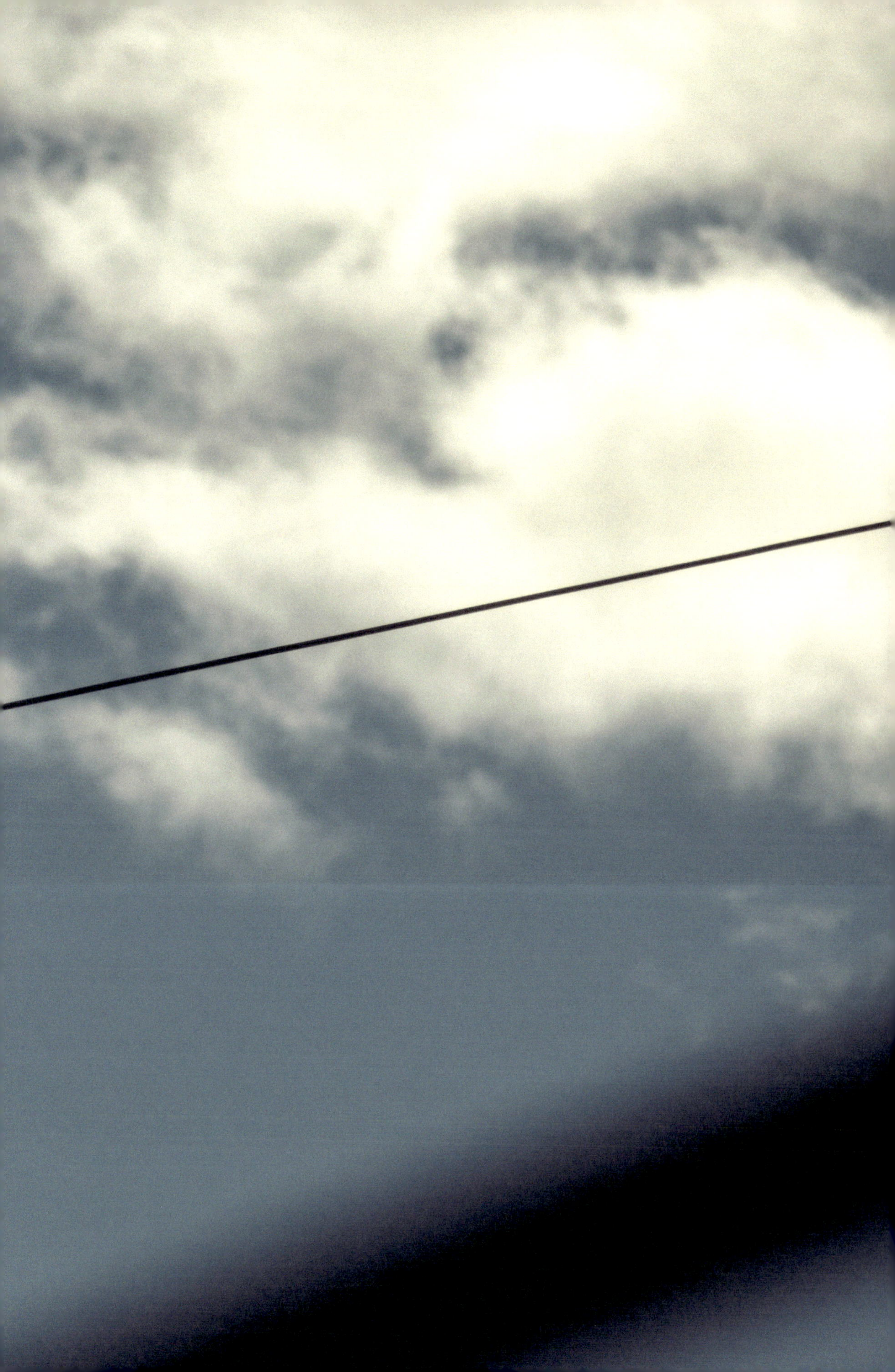

Juan Santamaria International Airport (SJO)

2 hr 21 min / 116 km

La Fortuna

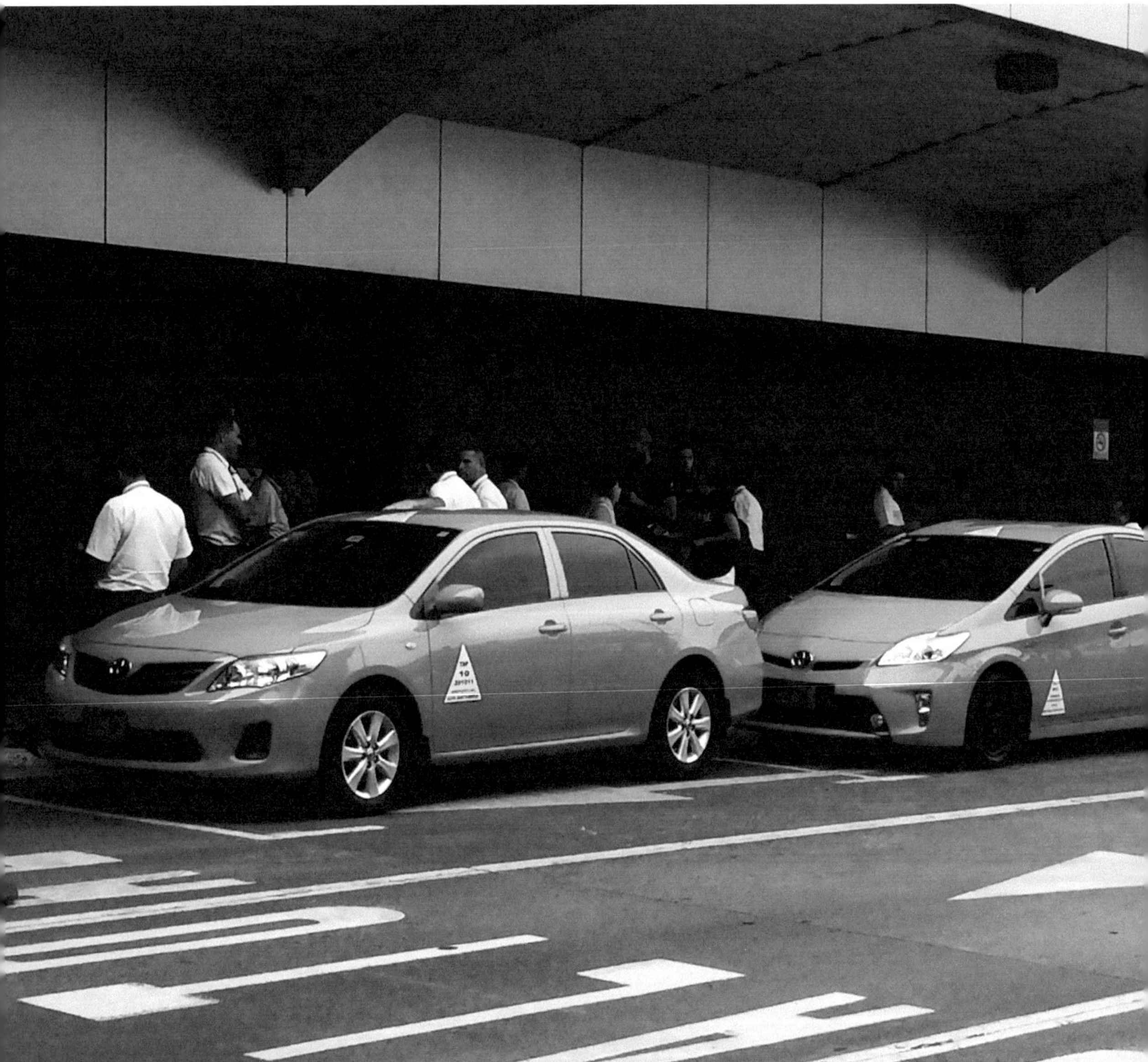

Journeying to the Past

As the sun peeked over the horizon, our plane touched down on the bustling tarmac of San Jose's international airport. By 8 a.m., we strolled out of the customs gate, welcomed by the cozy warmth of the tropical breeze wrapping around us.

Outside, the airport was alive with energy – a vibrant mix of eager faces, each one itching for their next big adventure. Among the crowd, a figure held up a sign with my name in bold letters – the telltale sign of our airport pickup arranged by the car rental company. For a moment, I couldn't help but feel a surge of importance, as if I were some distinguished VIP being whisked away to an exclusive destination. But as I stepped onto the pavement, reality came crashing down – the vehicle waiting for us was no sleek luxury sedan, but a humble seven-seater, patiently sharing its space with other travelers before our journey could begin.

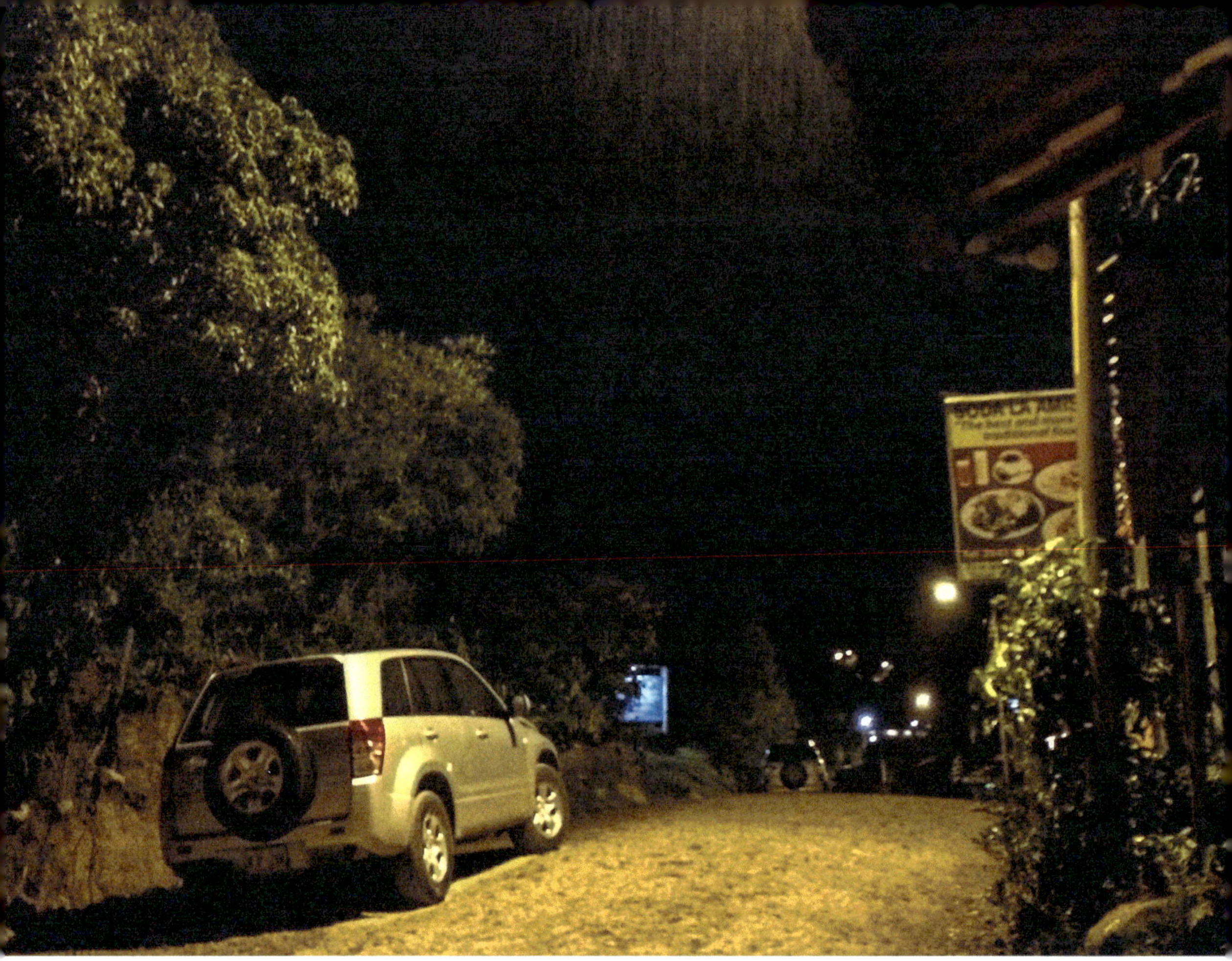

Embark on the adventure with today's version of 'Dai-fat-zai' by my side.

With a wry smile and a sense of humor about the situation, we piled into the practical ride, ready to embrace whatever adventures lay ahead, no matter how humble the transport may be. After all, isn't the journey half the fun?

Our little crew made its way to the car rental joint, guided by a chirpy lady who walked us through all the nitty-gritty rental stuff. We zipped through the paperwork, scribbled some signatures and dashed off to the parking lot to

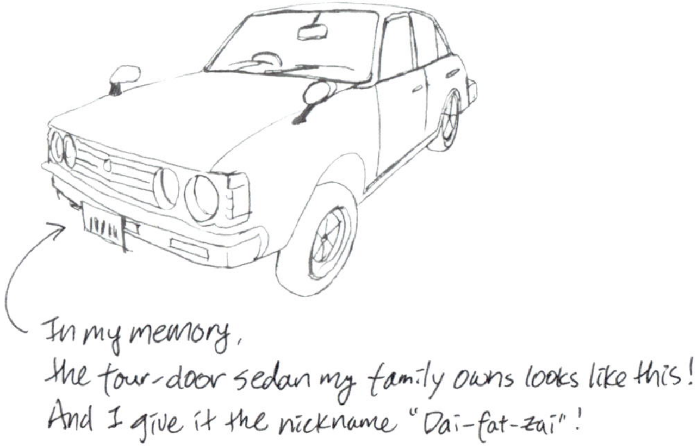

meet our ride – drumroll please – a Daihatsu Bego! Yup, a solid four-wheel drive ready to take us on our grand adventure!

The Daihatsu brand stirred up a wave of nostalgia from my childhood days. Back then, our family ran a small business, and we relied on a trusty Daihatsu sedan to get us through the daily grind. Despite bearing the marks of time and having changed hands multiple times, that car was the heart of our adventures.

Every morning, like clockwork, my brother would transform it into a makeshift cargo carrier, removing seats to make room for goods to be delivered. But by the afternoon, after completing our deliveries, the seats would magically reappear, and we'd pile into the car, ready for our beach escapades.

I can still vividly recall the excitement that bubbled up within me whenever my brother returned with the car, ready to whisk us away to the shore. "Dai-fat-zai is back, let's go swimming!" I'd shout with unbridled enthusiasm, eager to dive into the waves and soak up the sun.

Encountering the Daihatsu brand in a foreign land after all these years brought forth a flood of memories and unexpected surprises. It was like reconnecting with an old friend in an unfamiliar setting, a comforting reminder of the simple joys of yesteryears.

Back in the present moment, the car rental attendant tossed me the keys with a grin, pointing towards a modest white vehicle and declaring, "This is the one!" I couldn't help but raise an eyebrow in surprise. The car before me didn't exactly scream "adventure-ready." It looked more like it would struggle with a speed bump, let alone a muddy road. I half-expected it to turn into a tricycle at the sight of a pebble!

Caught between the urge to upgrade to something sturdier and the reality of time ticking away, I watched as the attendant casually unlocked the car with an old-fashioned key – no fancy remote control here! With a roar, the engine came to life, and a warning about returning the tank full echoed in my ears.

I hopped in, noting the odometer's impressive mileage – this car had definitely seen its fair share of road trips. A quick check confirmed everything was in working order, so I pushed thoughts of upgrades aside and instead asked about nearby grub spots. The attendant gestured towards a nearby shack, mentioning they all grabbed a bite there.

Excitedly, I headed over, greeted by the simplicity of the menu – beans, sausages, eggs, and coffee or tea. Figuring I'd go local, I ordered coffee and sausage with eggs. What arrived seemed like it had survived a culinary explosion – the sausage had burst, and the bread and eggs looked a tad dehydrated. Alas, this breakfast... well! Perhaps airplane meals weren't as shabby after all!

After inhaling the breakfast, I hopped back into the "Dai-fat-zai" (as I'd affectionately dubbed it) and hit the road. As we merged onto the highway, I couldn't shake the feeling of floating on clouds. This wasn't your typical road trip – it was more like a gentle drift. With a couple of hours until La Fortuna, I settled in, ready to embrace the unconventional journey ahead!

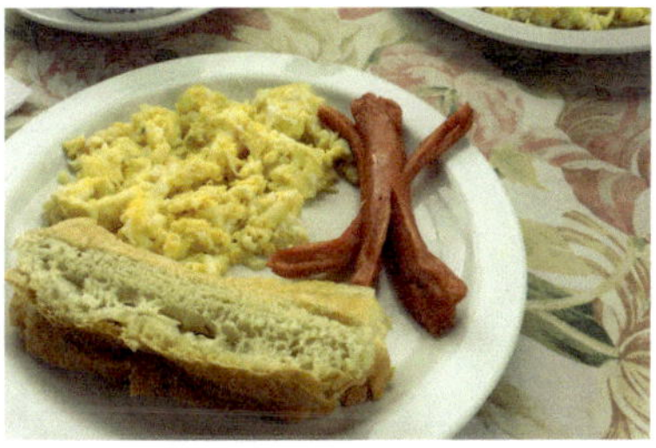

Culinary explosion breakfast!

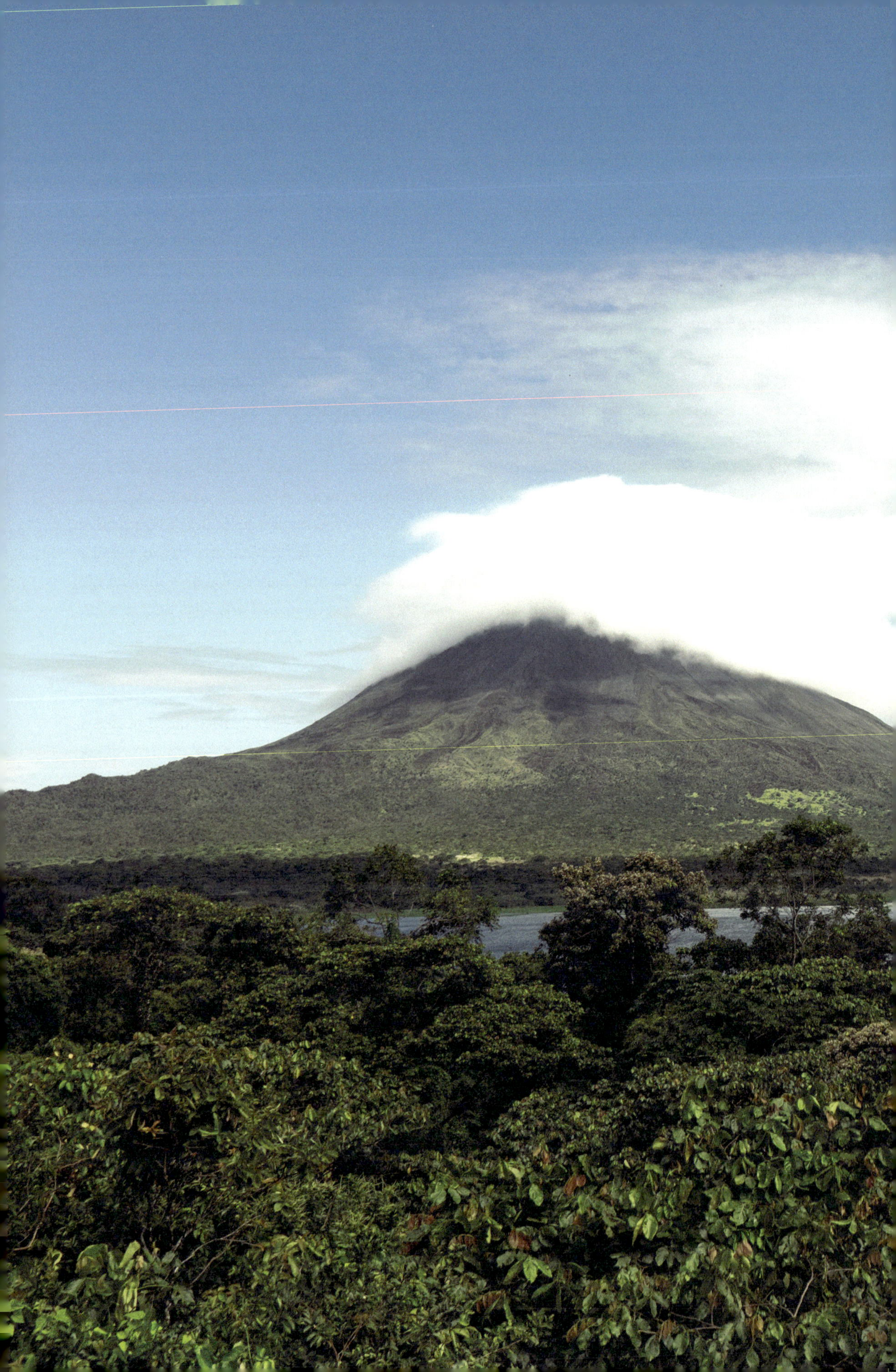

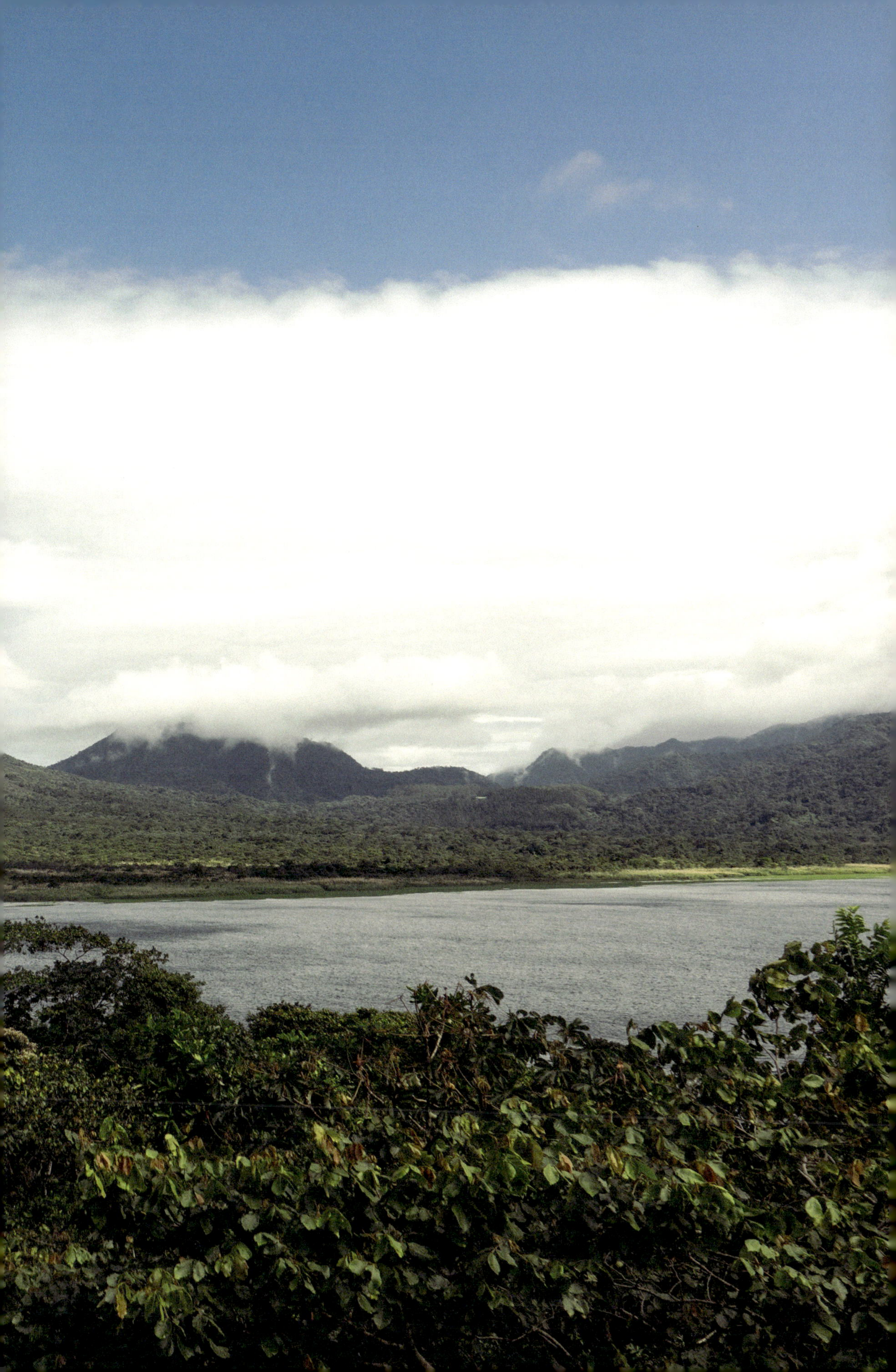

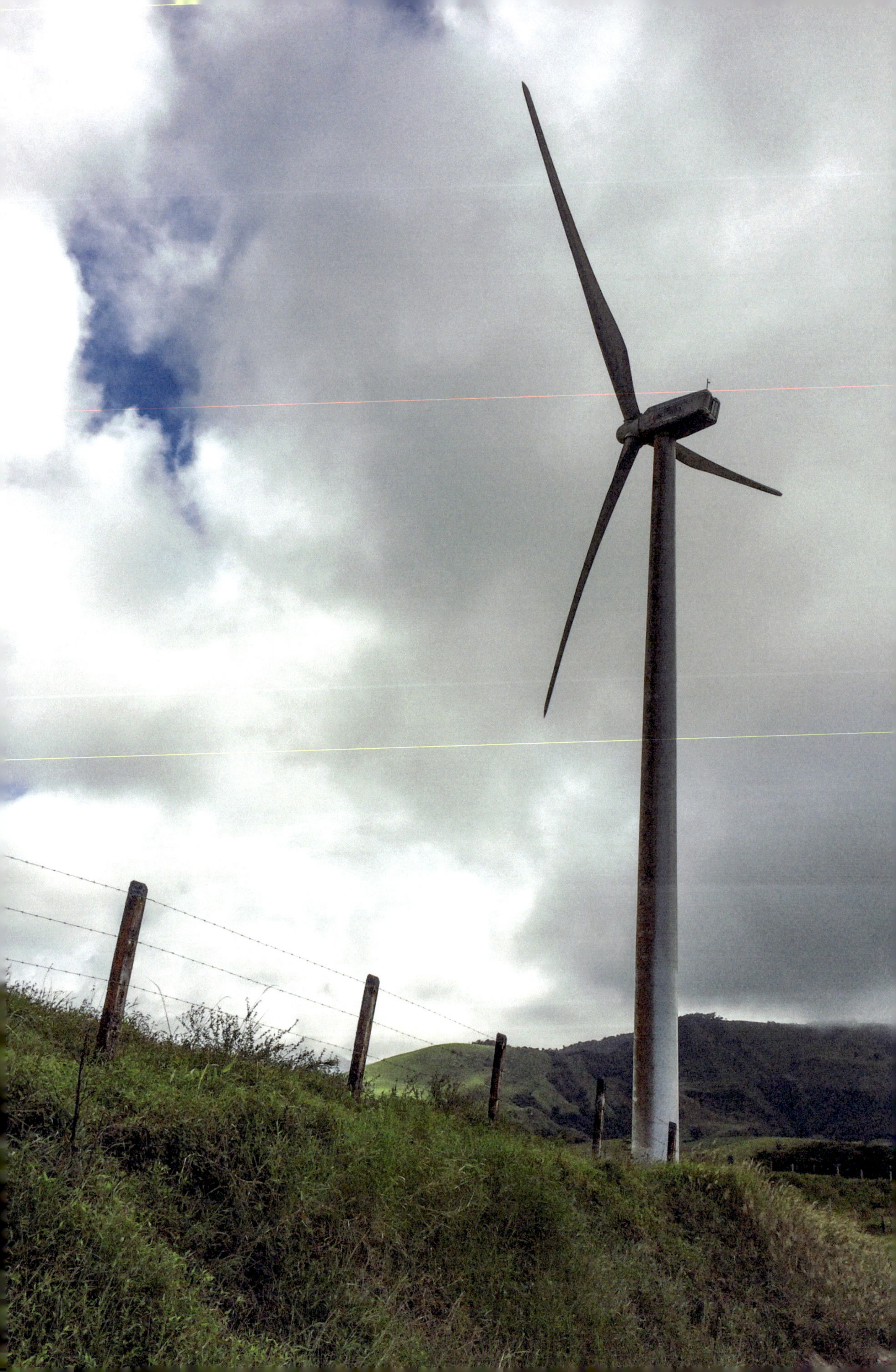

Swing with me "Dai-fat-zai"

In the lush landscapes of Costa Rica, where nature paints the sky with its vibrant hues, a story unfolds in the whispers of late November. Unlike the hustle and bustle of the peak tourist season from mid-December to April, this time of year tiptoes on the edge of the dry season's farewell. It's a moment when occasional rain kisses the earth, and the tourist crowds thin, offering solace to those like myself who prefer to steer clear of the bustling masses.

As our trusty Dai-fat-zai meandered down the road, the relentless sun played a game of hide-and-seek with us. I slipped on my favorite shades, welcomed the cool breeze of the air conditioner, and let the tunes of '80s pop songs from a local radio station carry me away. It felt like stepping into a time machine to some distant, foreign land. An hour's drive took us from the main road to a smaller path, turning our smooth ride into a bumpy dance on the weathered asphalt.

Above us, a thick blanket of clouds cleverly shielded the sun from view. Approaching our destination, the low-pressure clouds sprinkled a gentle drizzle, cloaking the landscape in a mystical mist. Peering through the car window was like watching an old black-and-white movie on a vintage TV with dancing snowflakes.

Following the guidance of Google Maps, a right turn at the next intersection led us to La Fortuna Street. Though the sky remained overcast, the rain had eased. Turning onto the street revealed a majestic mountain in the distance, its peak concealed by thick gray clouds—the infamous Arenal Volcano. Standing tall at 5,437 feet, this active volcano had a tumultuous history, with a significant eruption devastating lives and villages in 1968. Despite subsequent lava flows and rock ejections, the volcano remained awake until 2010. Scientists continued to label Arenal Volcano as active.

La Fortuna emerged as a hotspot, offering many activities like ziplining, canyoning, and white-water rafting. The town's volcanic perks extended to the best hot springs around. At its

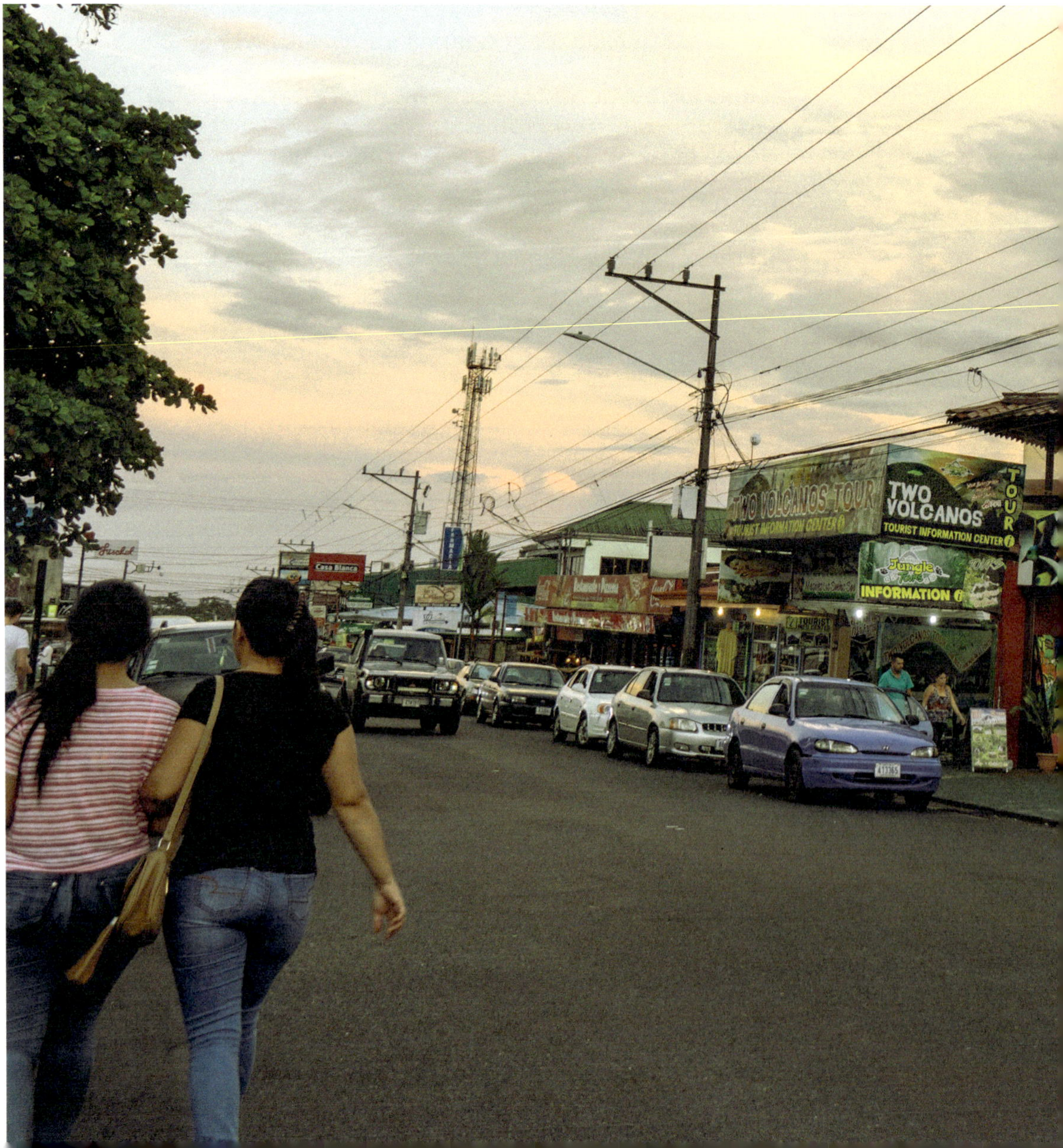

heart lay a church, surrounded by bustling streets lined with small hotels, eateries, and tourist services. My chosen 2.5-star hotel is nestled conveniently behind a quaint square. Despite its peaceful vibe, the location provided easy access to the town's pulse. Parking Dai-fat-zai in the hotel garden, I entered the reception area, where the front desk clerk, mid-lunch, greeted me warmly. Amid his bites, he efficiently checked me in, patiently answering my questions about dinner spots and recent weather changes. The locals' warmth became tangible in just a few hours, from the car rental to the hotel, deepening my fondness for this charming place. It was clear that a delightful place must indeed house lovely people, and my affection for this town gem grew stronger.

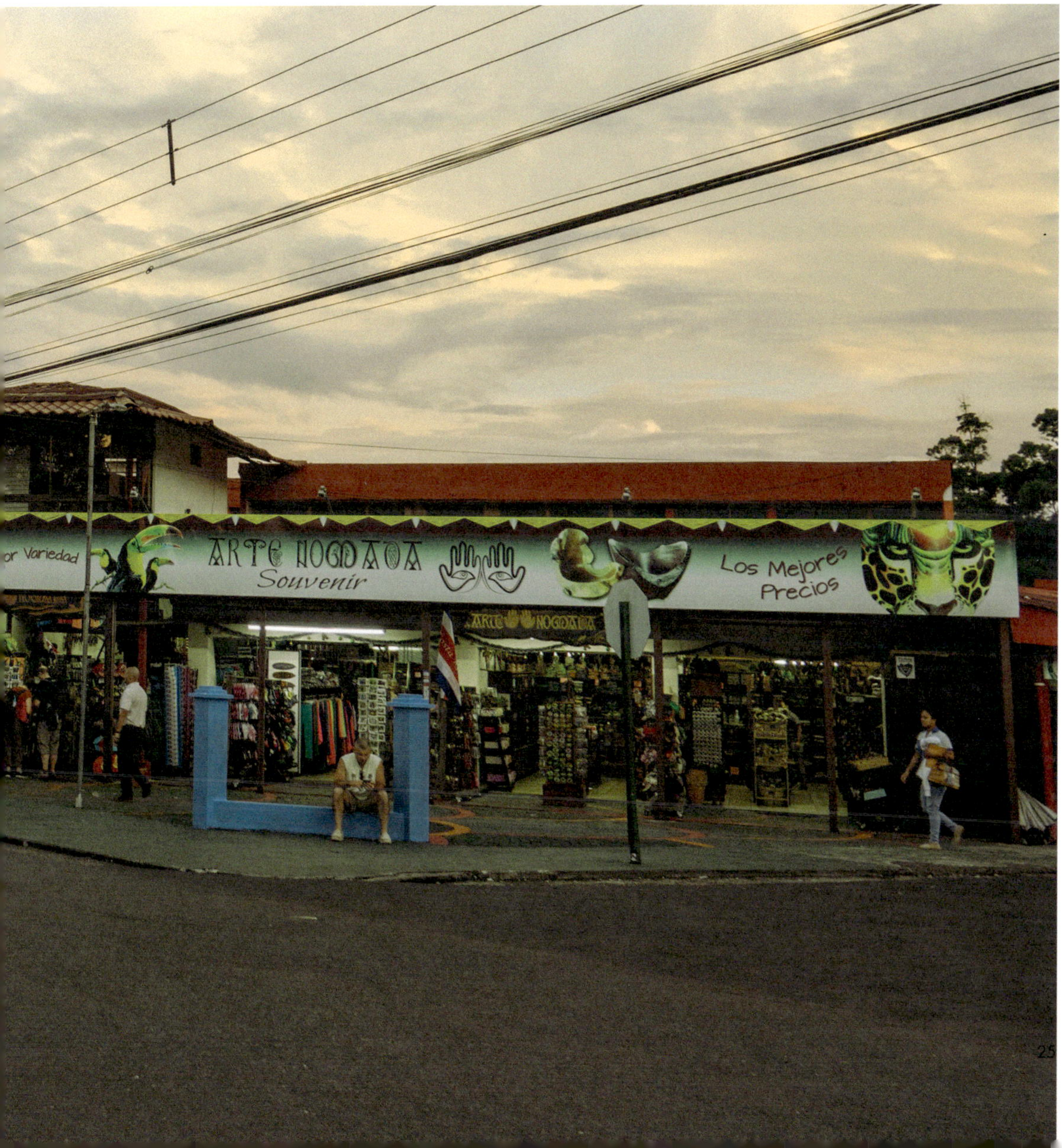

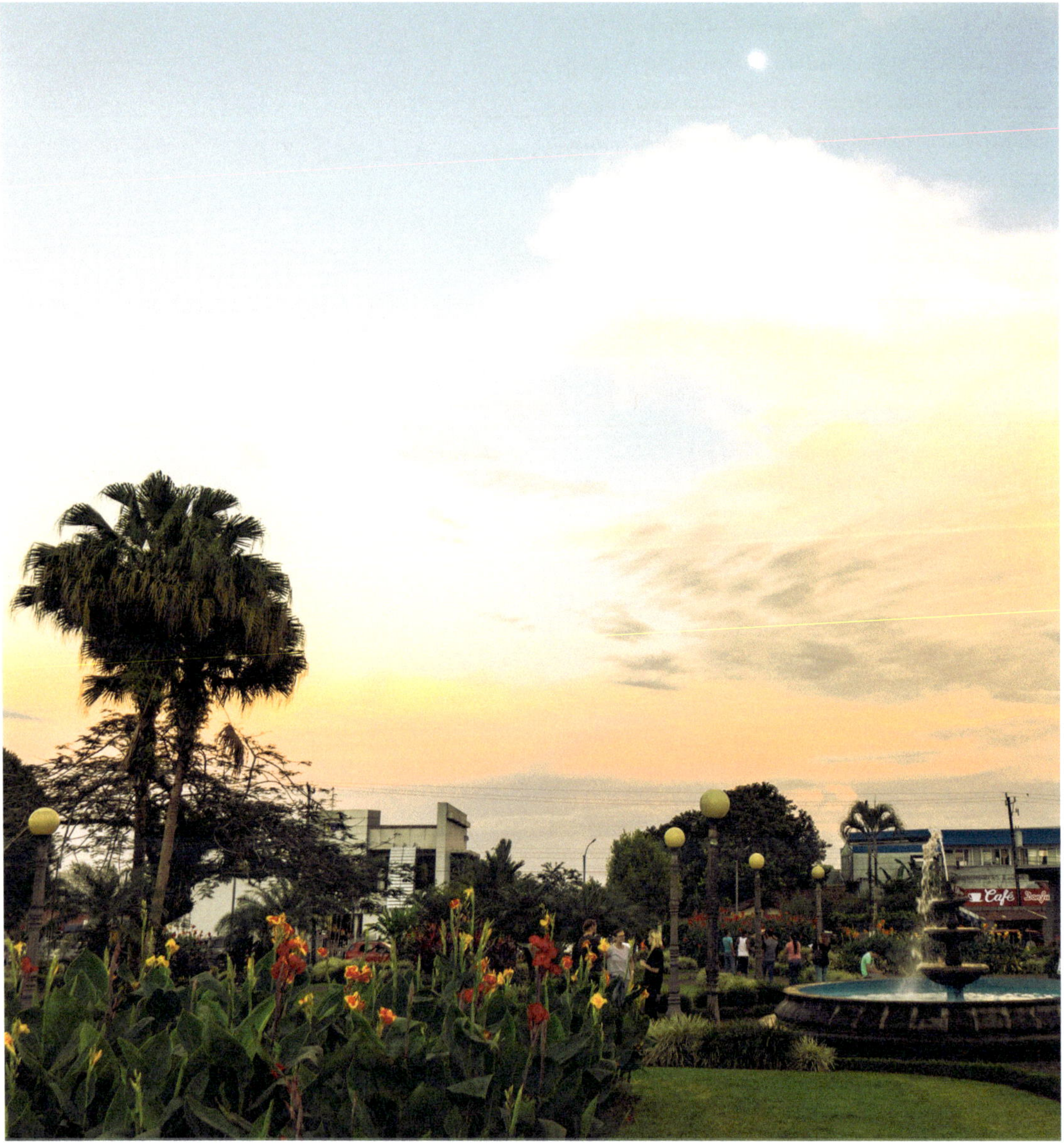
Café

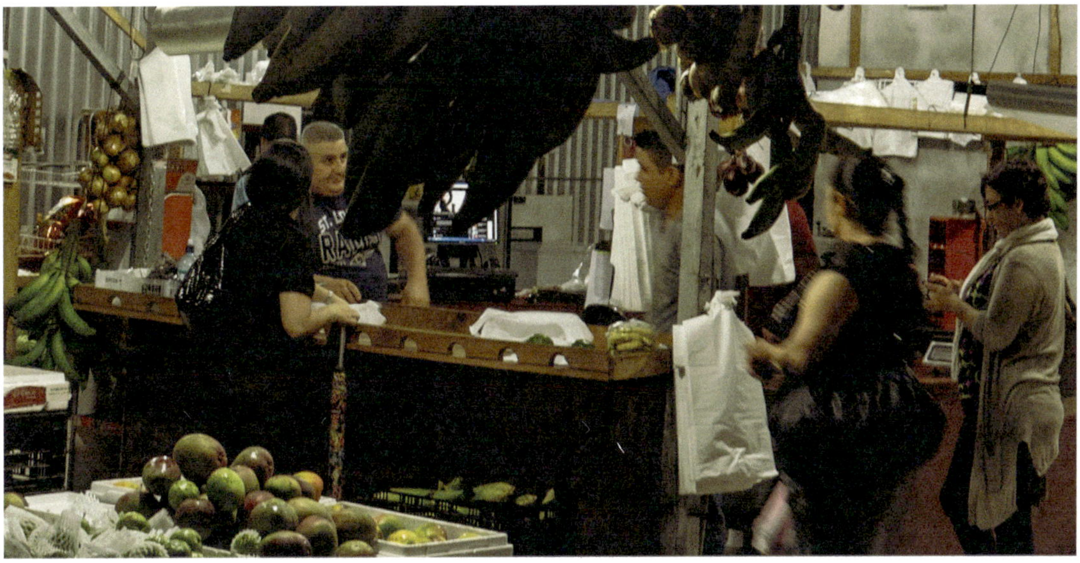

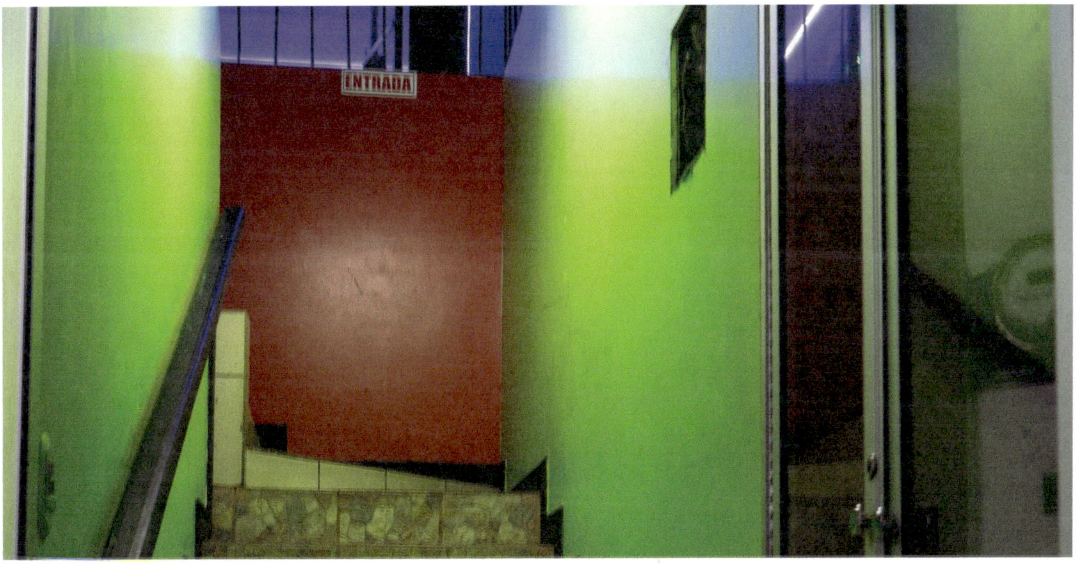
ENTRADA

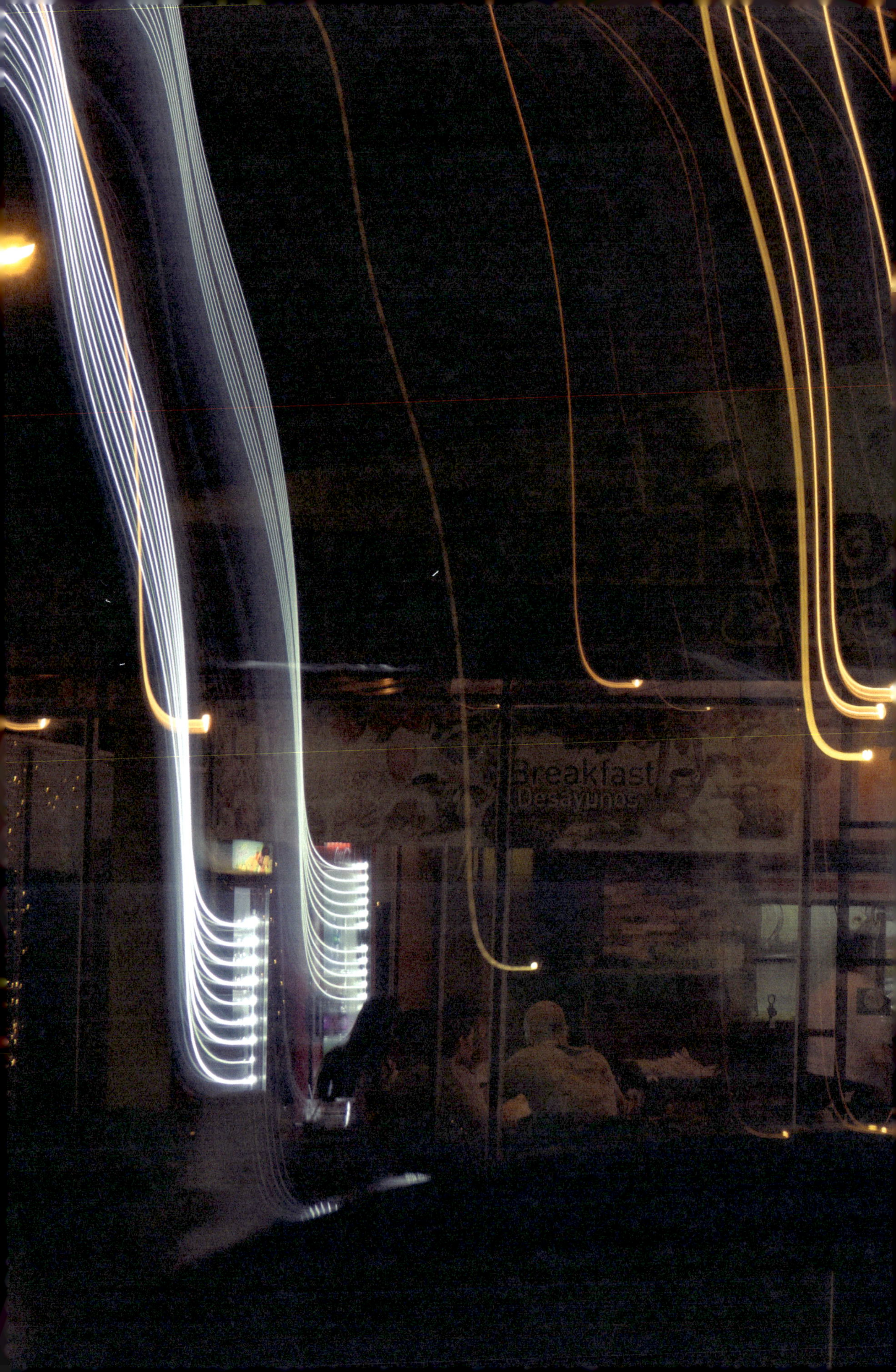
Breakfast
Desayunos

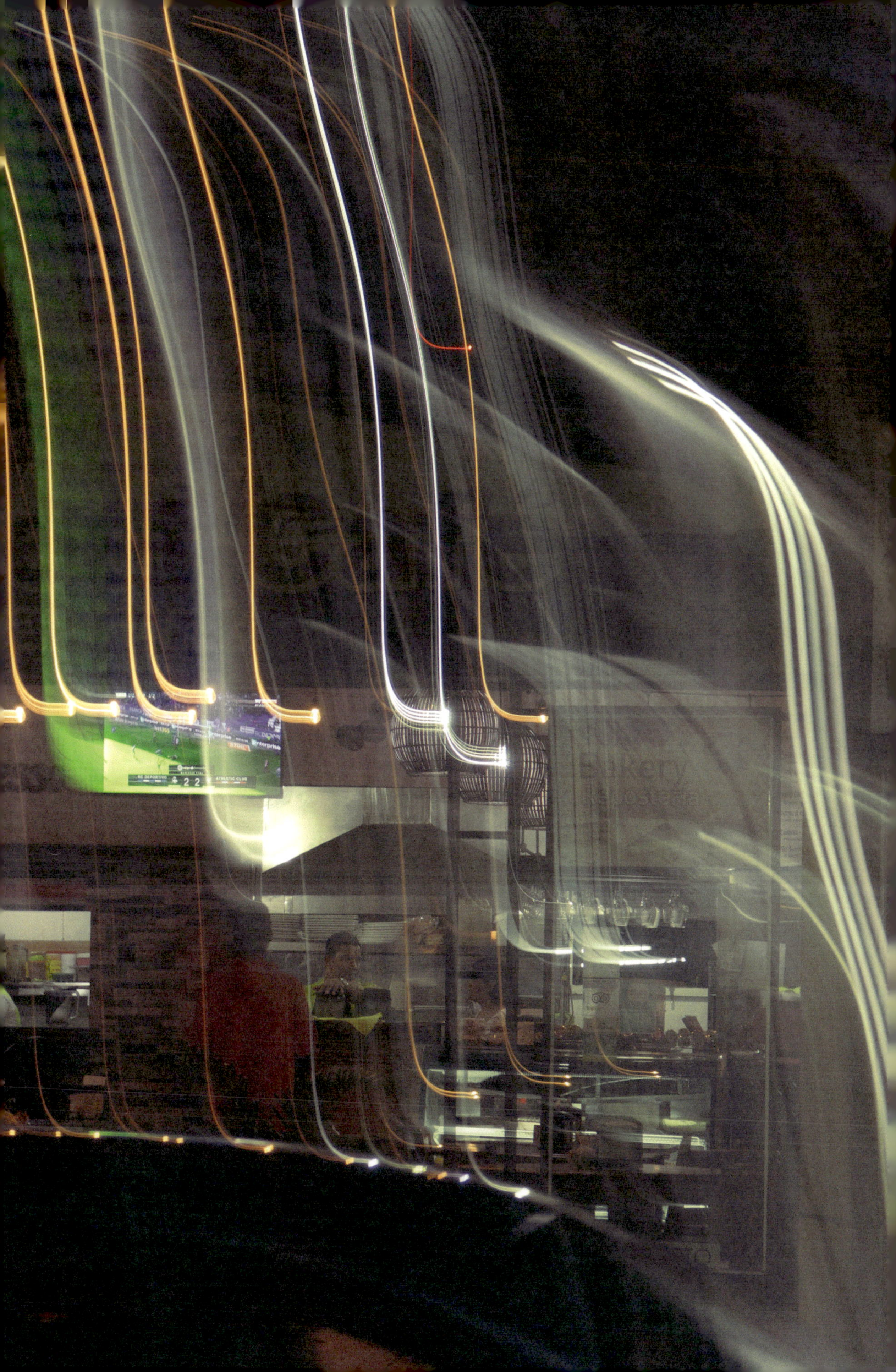
RC DEPORTIVO
2 2
ATHLETIC CLUB
enterprise

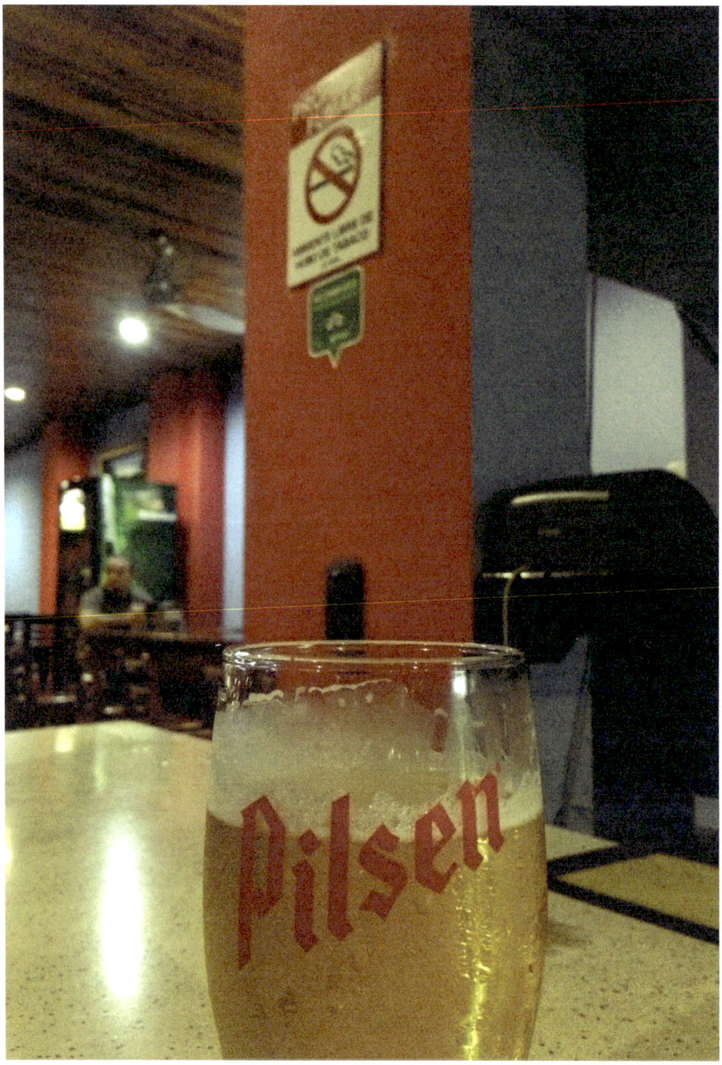
Pilsen

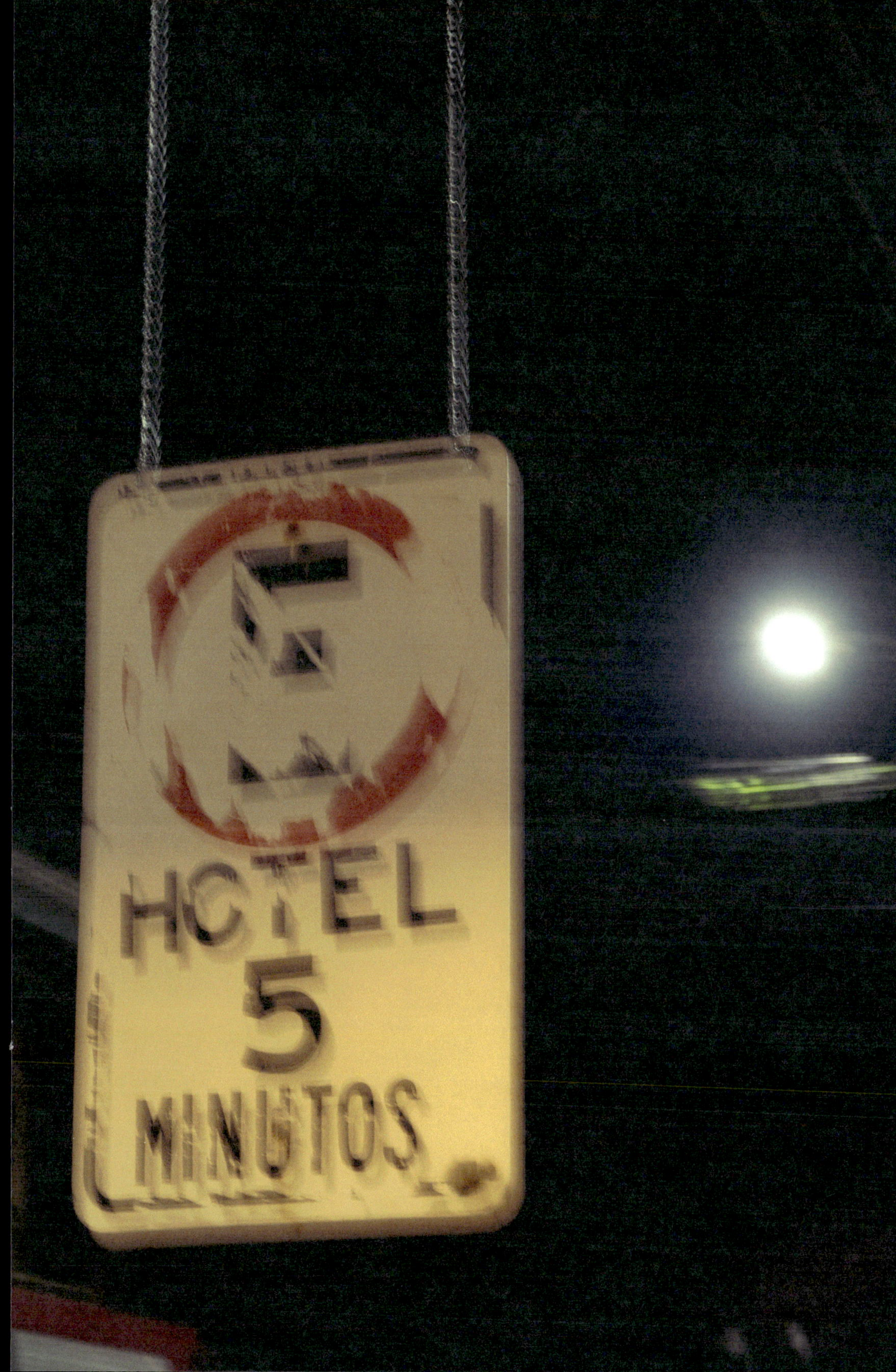
HOTEL
5
MINUTOS

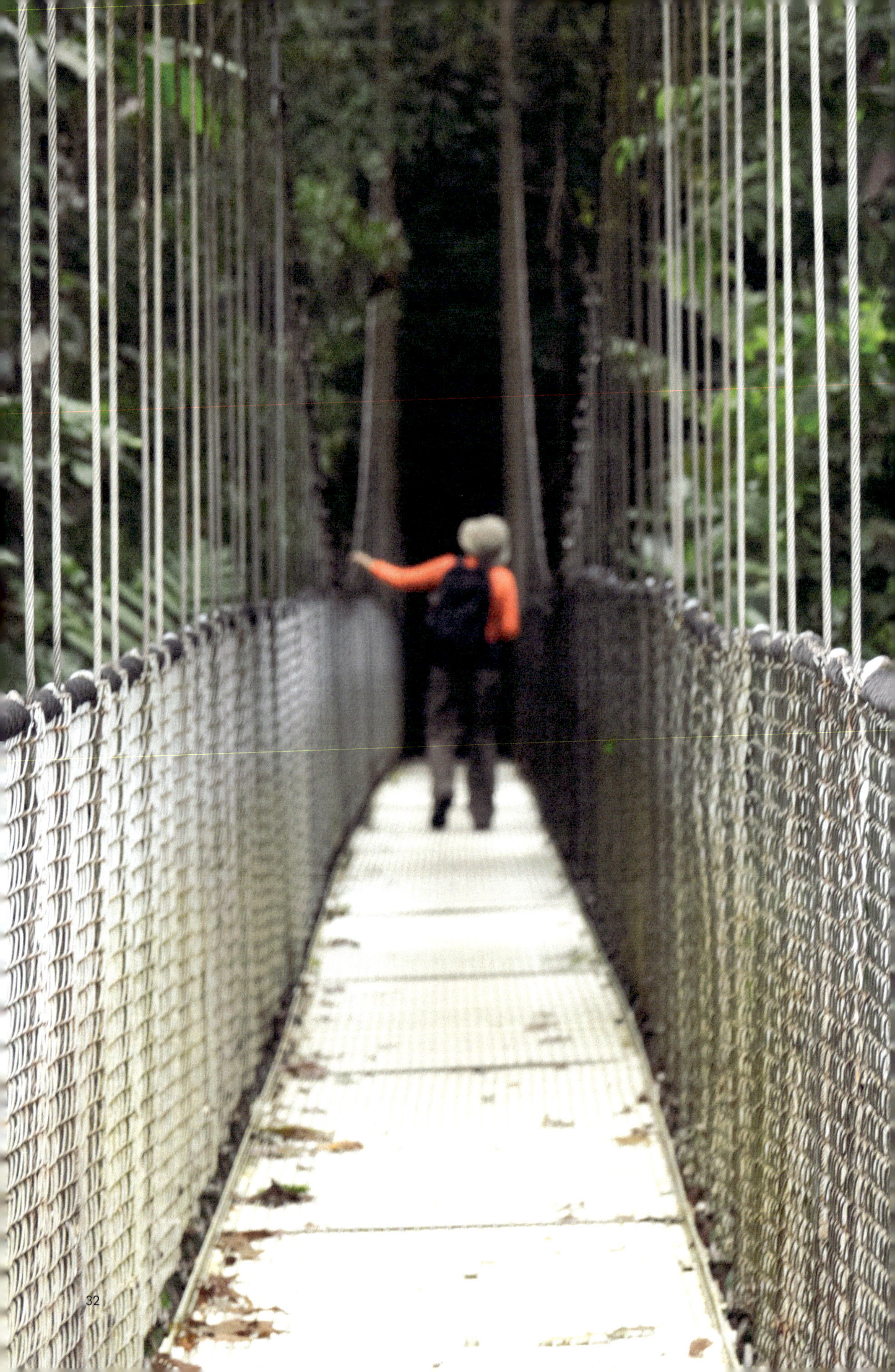

Whether in Sunshine or Rain

Rainforest Canopy Bridge

Stepping into the hotel, a peculiar sense of nostalgia washes over me—it's like a journey back in time. The small rooms are adorned with a distinct 1960s charm. A fan dangles lazily from the ceiling, surrounded by simple wooden chairs, crisp white sheets, and an unexpected guest—a frog made from neatly folded towels, complete with big eyes and red lips, perched on the bed. It's quirky, but it adds to the charm. Despite the slightly weathered bathroom, it passes my germaphobe inspection. Once my modest luggage finds its spot, I venture out, eager to explore the tropical rainforest by crossing the suspension bridge.

So, there I was, ready to dive into the Arenal Hanging Bridges Park, a sprawling 600-acre wonderland. With its mountain trail decked out with 15 bridges, spanning a total distance of 3.1 kilometers, it's shaping up to be quite the adventure. With a leisurely 2.5-hour stroll on the agenda, I'm psyched for some up-close wildlife encounters amid the lush tropical rainforest.

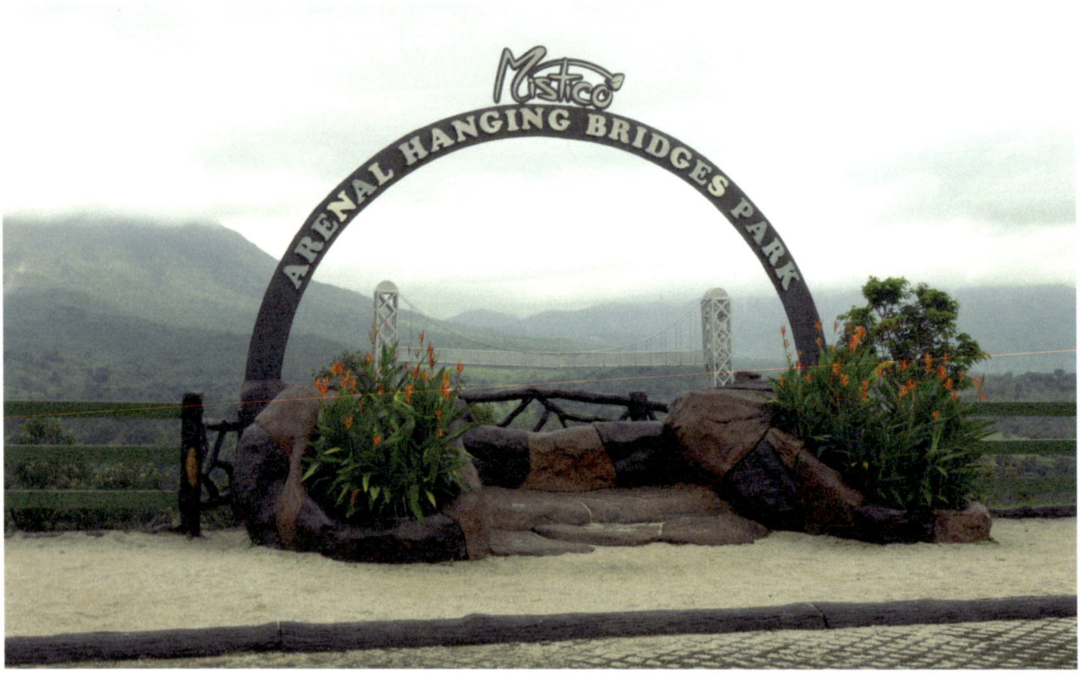

Místico Arenal Hanging Bridges

https://www.misticopark.com/

Now, imagine being surrounded by towering mountains, with the park's colossal landmark standing tall in the background. Beyond that, as far as the eye can see, stretches an endless sea of forest. Sure, gray clouds are hugging the volcano's summit, hiding the blue sky, but trust me, the vibrant greenery steals the show. Standing there, taking it all in, I'm mesmerized by the panorama of sky, mountains, and forests. And let's not forget the occasional bird fluttering by, adding to the whole enchanting scene. Plus, the moist air? It's like a shot of energy, making every sense tingle with excitement and leaving me grinning from ear to ear.

Let the adventure begin!

The mountain trail embarks on a flat, narrow road, then slowly winds its way up a gentle slope, with plants all around. The flora in this tropical rainforest is something else—huge tree trunks covered in wet moss, with water droplets glistening and insects doing their little dance. It's like a whole mini-world for these tiny creatures! Ever wonder what it's like to live life on a tree trunk? Well, here's your chance to find out!

Navigating the mountain path, I traverse several small suspension bridges before reaching the grandeur of a longer one. As I gaze upon it, an unexpected encounter awaits—a solitary figure walking toward me from the opposite side of the bridge. We meet briefly at the center, but he hurries on, reaching the other side before turning around and vanishing into the mountain path. I pause, standing in the middle of the bridge, observing the dense woods with branches and green leaves swaying in the wind. Closing my eyes, I embrace the breeze's melody. Upon reopening them, the dancing forest remains, revealing the distant mountains and sky beyond.

Our trek through the tropical rainforest continues, including numerous suspension bridges. We pay close attention to the towering trees and the forest's inhabitants, yet nothing reveals itself along the way. Until a bend in the road unveils two figures standing still. They turn, offering a quiet gesture upon hearing my footsteps.

"There's a little bird on that branch!" one of them whispers.

"Which branch? What kind of bird?" I asked.

"Look at the three big leaves in front of you and the trunk stretching behind the smaller leaves. That little bird is standing right here!"

"What kind of bird? I can't see it!"

"It just turned around, and now only its colorful body is visible, its head hidden by the branch!"

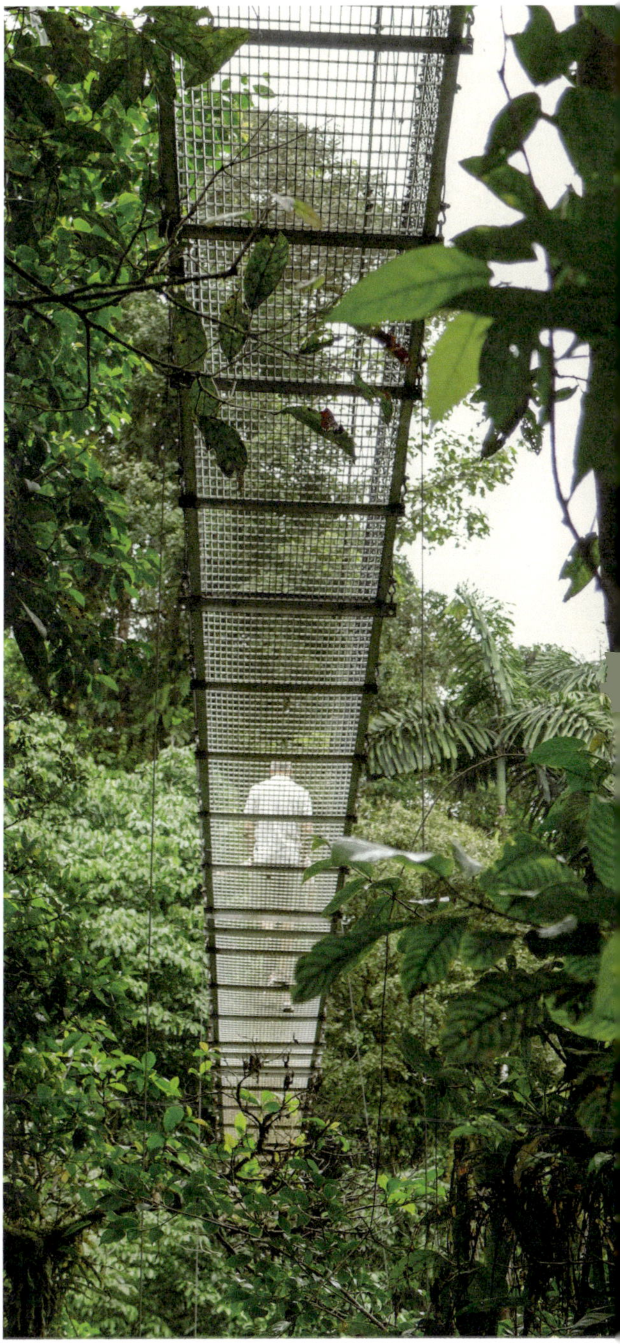

Even as I utter, 'Is it that plump, rotund red body...,' the fluttering sound of wings abruptly interrupts. With its transient beauty, the exquisite bird vanishes into the forest, leaving us with a feeling of time lost.

Reflecting on the just-traversed suspension bridge, be it long or short, it feels like a chapter in life. There were chance encounters that didn't lead to acquaintance; there were beautiful moments brushed aside. Whether leisurely strolling to appreciate or hastily passing by, either closely enjoying or gazing into the distance, whether in sunshine or rain – each step seemed to encapsulate a unique episode of life.

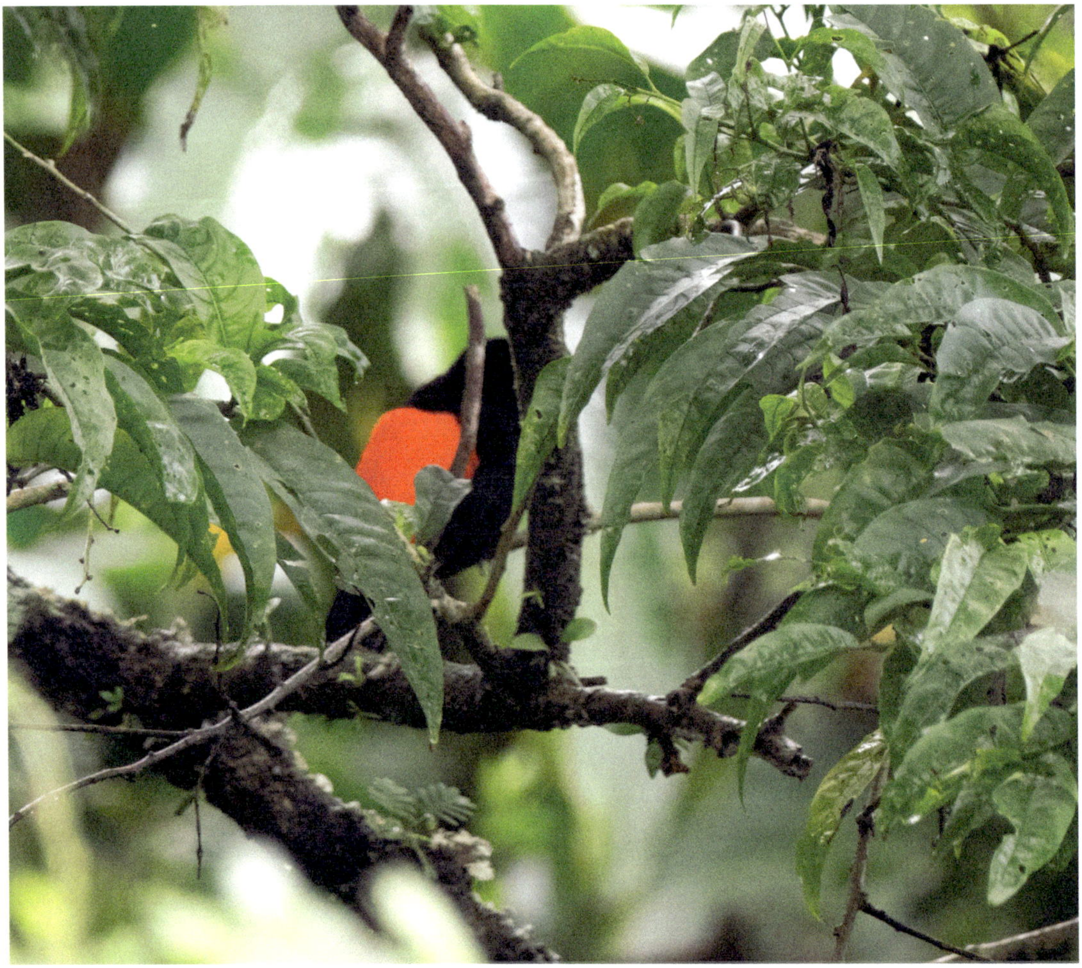

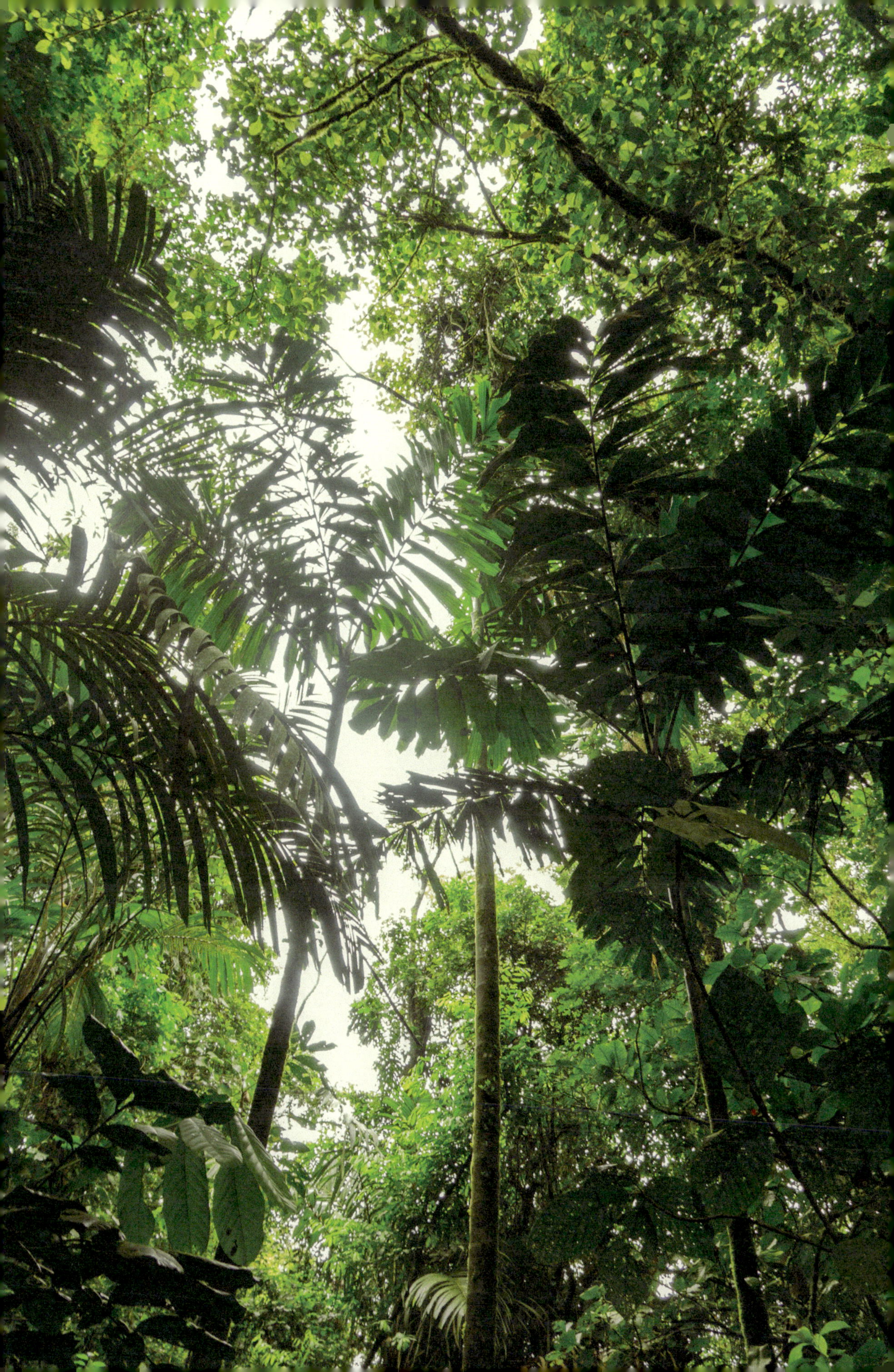

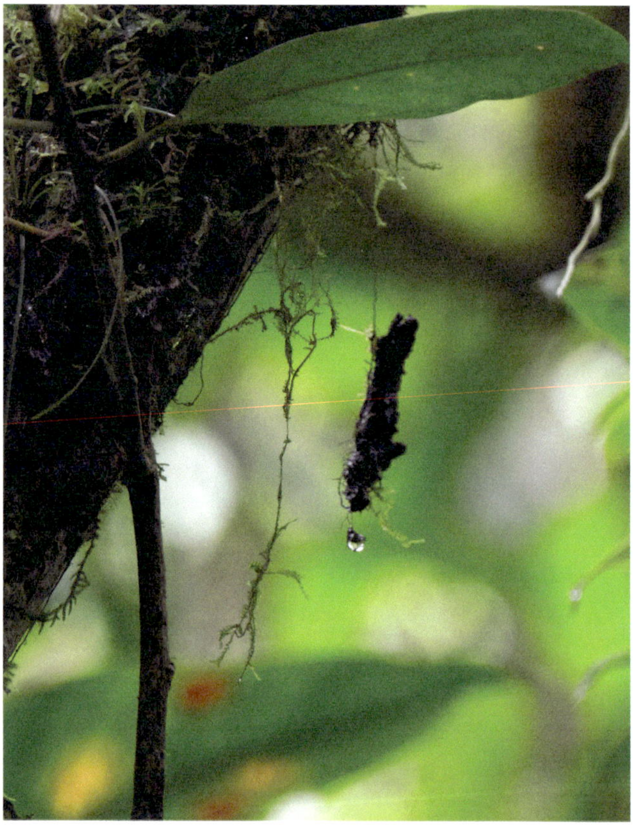

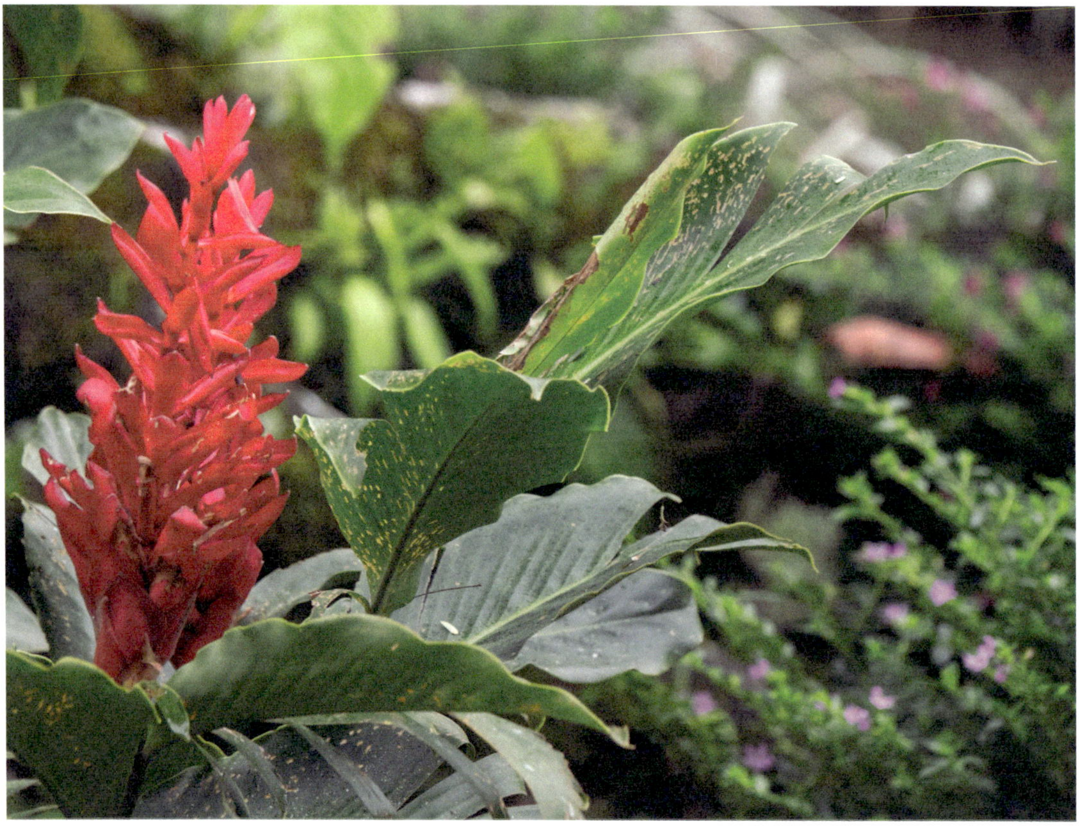

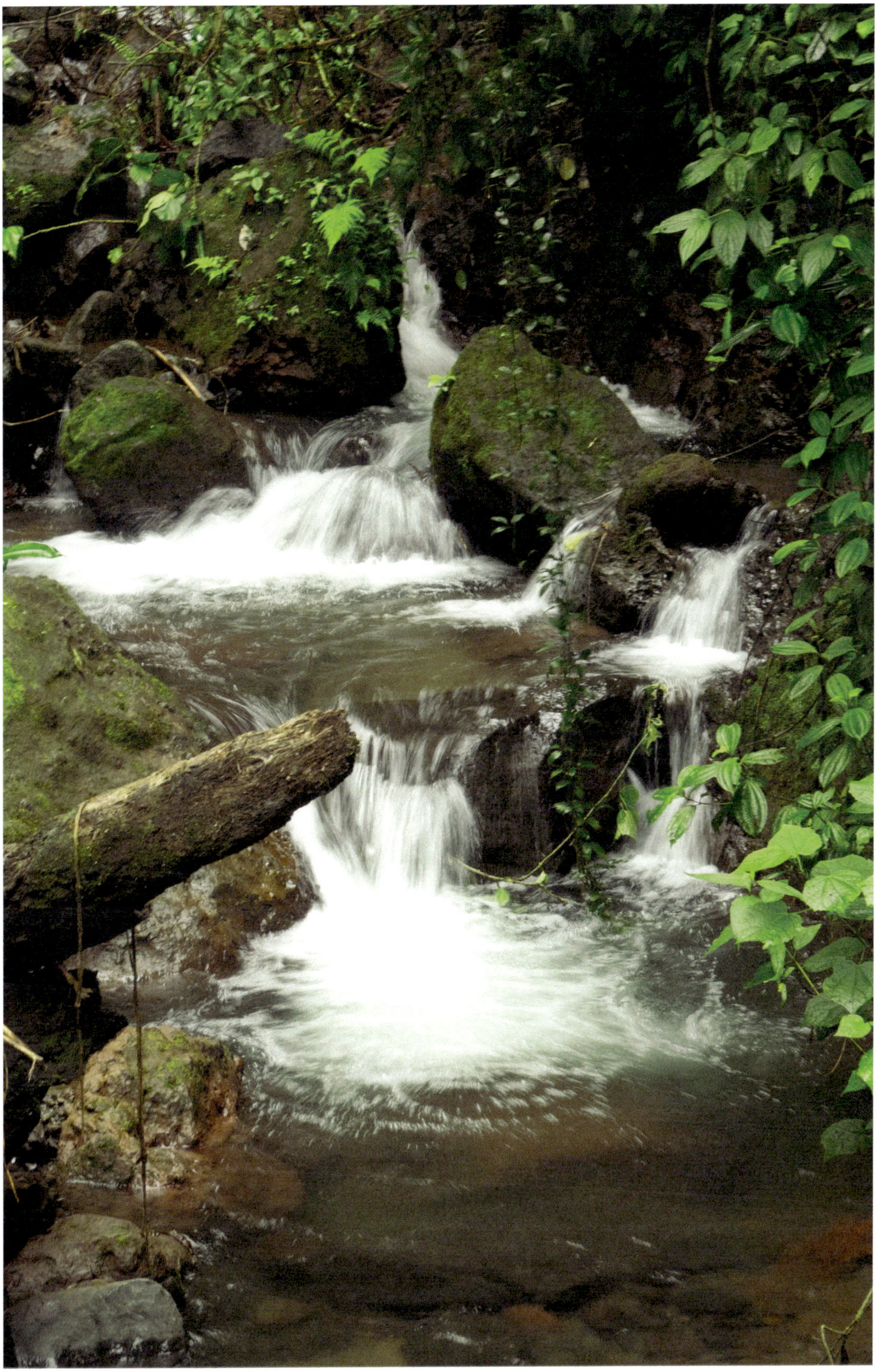

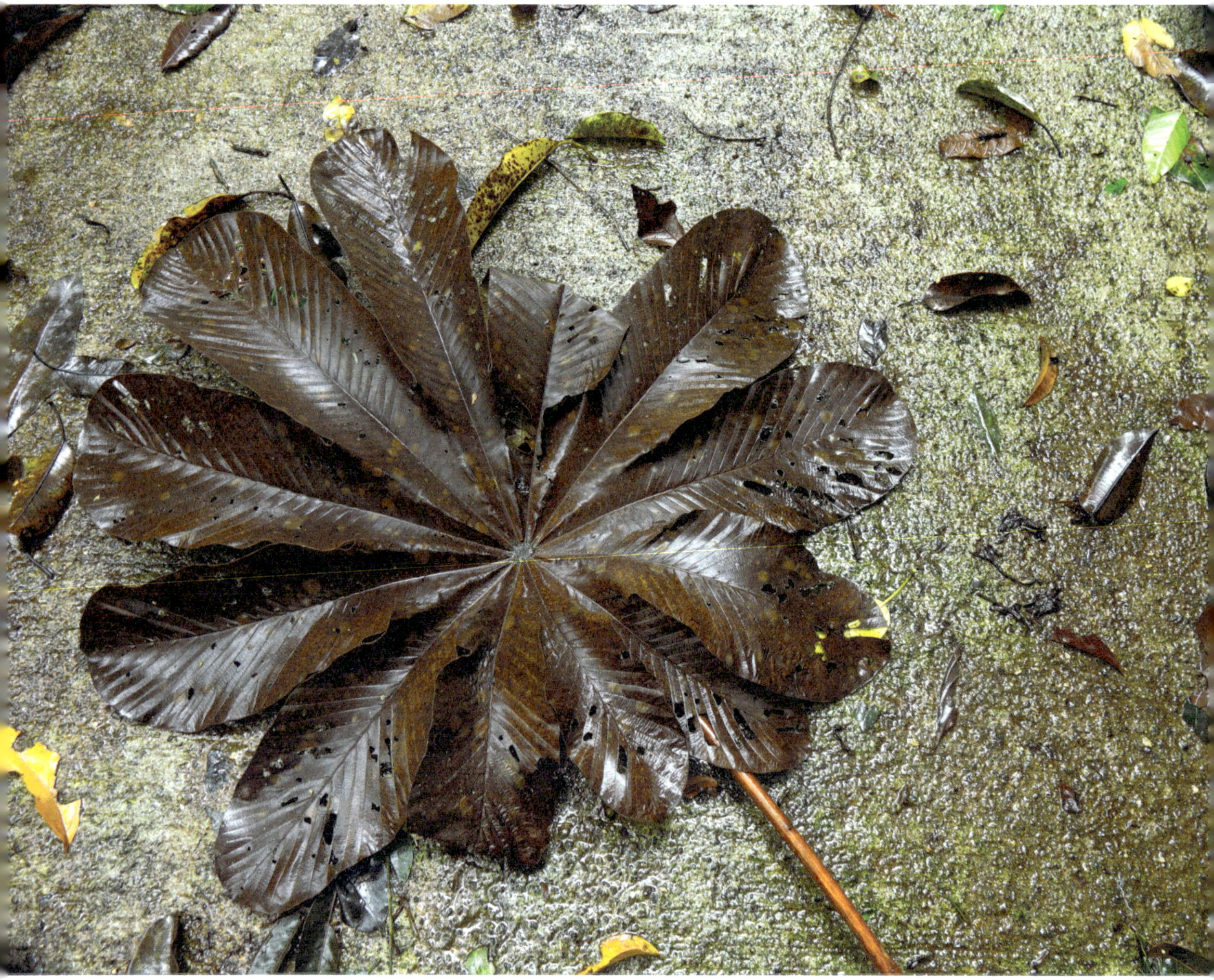

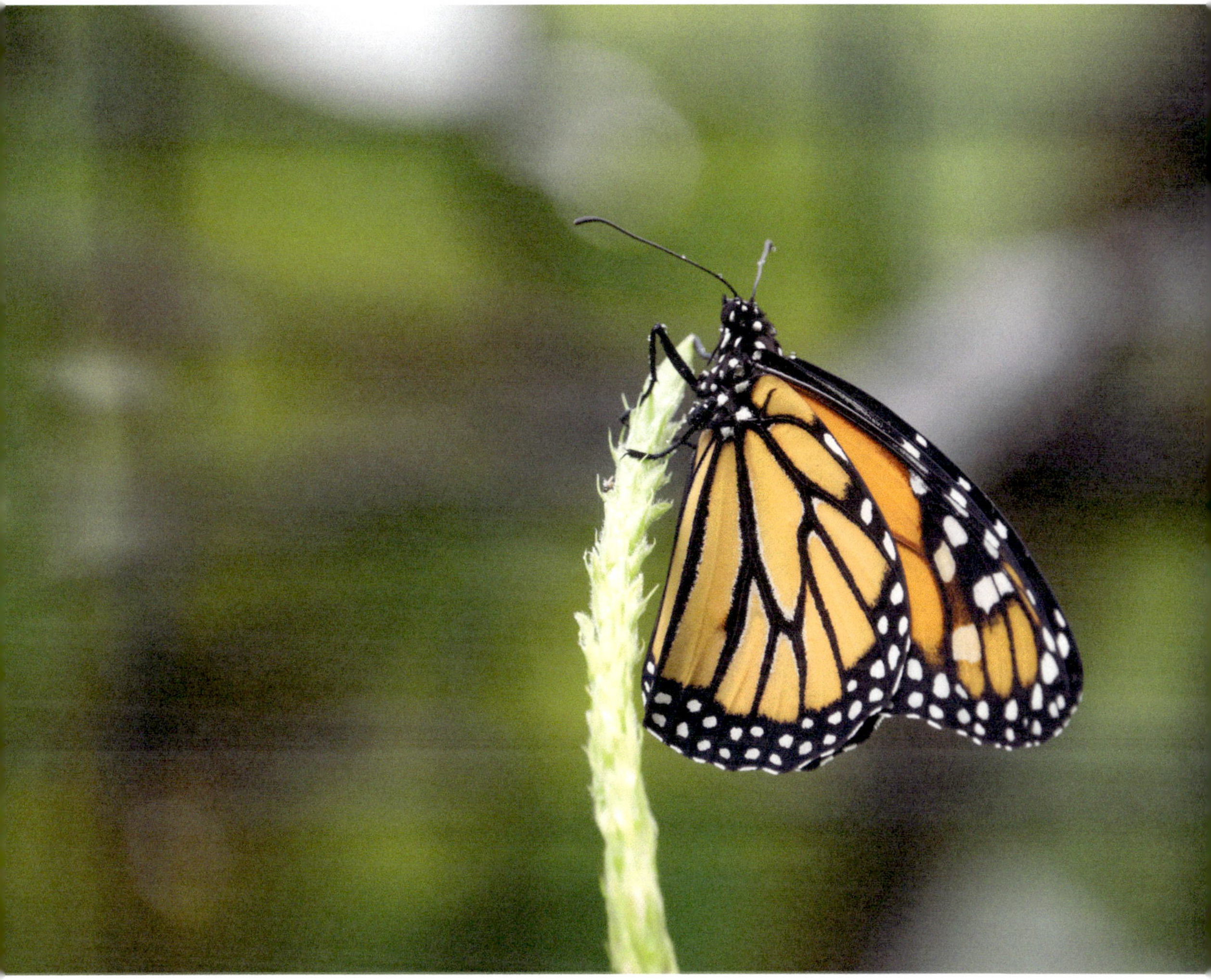

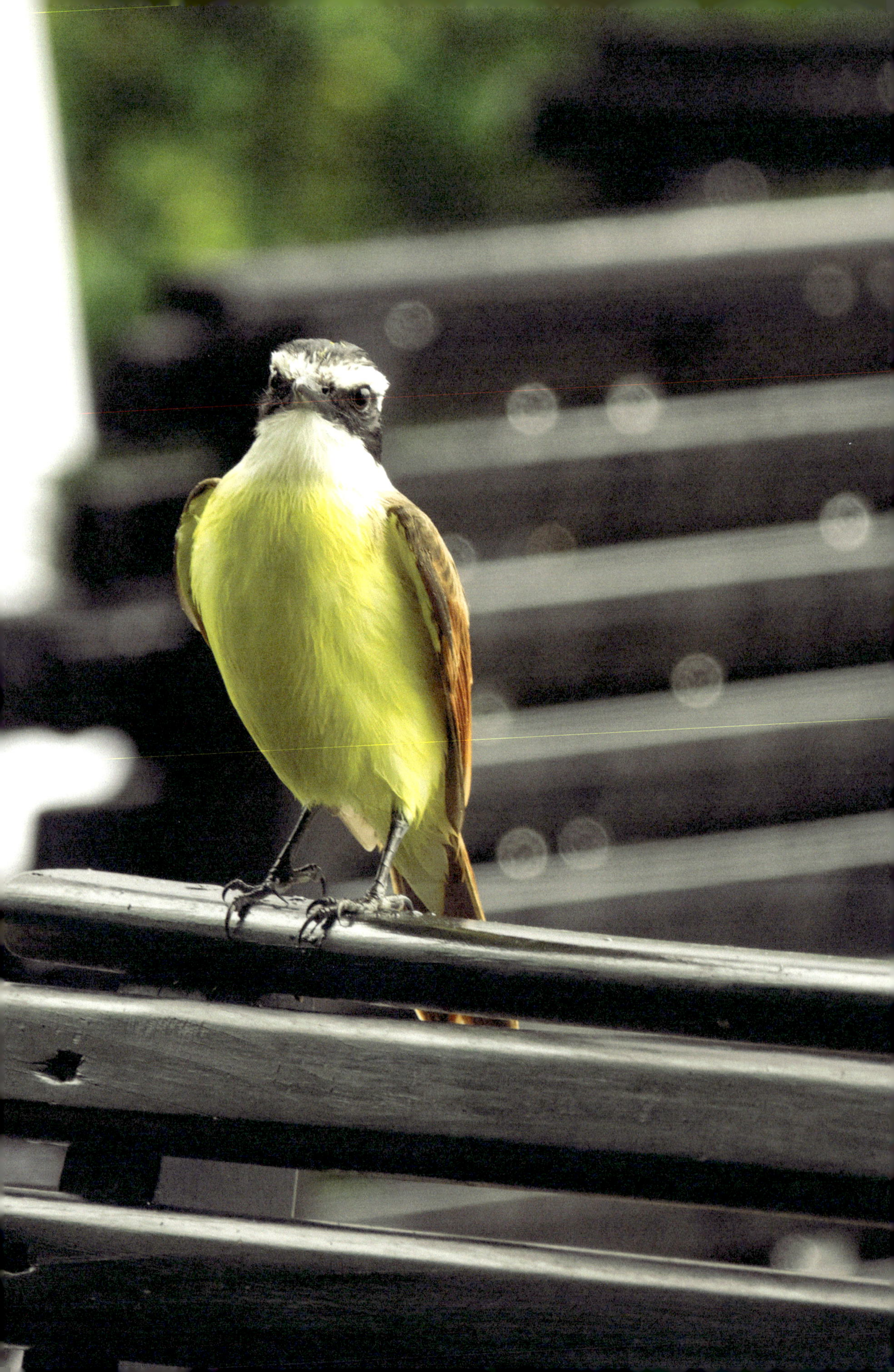

Enchanting River Rainfall

Picture this: this morning, I'm chilling in the hotel garden, munching on breakfast, and the weather decides to put on a show. There's this light drizzle, nothing too serious, just enough to add a bit of magic to the scene. And oh boy, those clouds above, they're teasing us like they might unleash a real downpour any moment.

Anyway, while I'm sipping my coffee, I notice these birds putting on a show of their own. They're darting around, playing tag in the sky like they don't have a care in the world. Eventually, a couple of them decide to take a pit stop on a bench nearby. They shake off the rain like it's no big deal, take a breather, then off they go again into the rainy abyss. It's like they're dancing to the rhythm of the raindrops, right?

After breakfast, it's time for some real adventure. We hop on this boat for what they call a "monkey tour" along the Rio Penas Blancas. The river winds its way through the Tilaran Mountain Range, offering some easy rapids for the thrill-seekers. But me? I'm all about that chill vibe, cruising along the tourist-friendly stretch where monkeys love to make an appearance. Let's see what the jungle has in store for us today!

Two young fellas, one looking like he's been around the block a few times leading the charge, and a fresh face, greeted me by a car decked out with an inflatable kayak strapped to the roof. Before we hit the road, the seasoned leader chimed in:

"Hey there! Just a heads up, the weather's not playing nice today. Heavy rain's in the forecast. Got yourself a windbreaker? It's gonna be handy. And a dry bag for your gear wouldn't hurt either!"

I nodded, saying, "Yeah, got my raincoat and windbreaker sorted. Camera's got a cover, but you know heavy rain can still be a bother."

"No sweat, mate. I've got a dry bag for you. Pop your camera in there when it starts pouring. Just so you know, my phone's gonna share the space, so treat it gentle," he warned me.

As the newbie at the wheel kicked off our journey, the seasoned pro kept the conversation flowing:

"So, the river we're cruising to is pretty chill. Me and my buddy here will handle the paddling. You just sit back, take in the sights. Although, gotta warn ya, this rain might keep some of the wildlife under wraps. But hey, let's roll with it and see what we stumble upon."

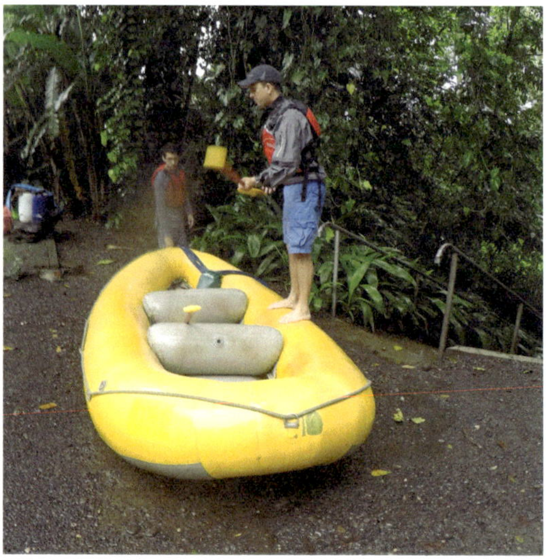

Alright, buckle up for a tale of destined encounters, even when we're a thousand miles apart. Let's dive into the adventure waiting for us today!

We pulled up to a wooded clearing, and our leader pointed us toward a hut to get fitted for life jackets. Meanwhile, they unloaded the inflatable kayak from the car roof. After a quick ten-minute session on life jacket positioning, we headed to the riverbank where the leader pointed out our ride:

"I'll get the kayak in the water from here, and then you folks can hop on!"

I eyed the narrow steps, bracing myself for a challenge. But much to my surprise, they effortlessly slid the kayak down horizontally on the handrail, making it look like child's play.

As I geared up to board, I couldn't help but notice the river's unexpected turbulence—mild rapids, swirling yellow water. The leader and

Peñas Blancas River Safari Float

https://jacamartours.com/tours/arenalvolcano/penas-blancas-river-safari-float/

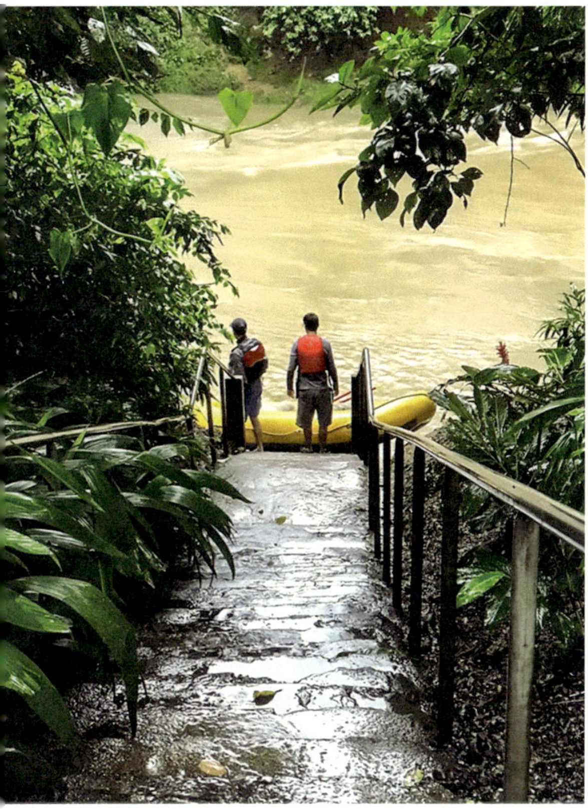

I squinted, spotting numerous tiny dots, smaller than fists, neatly arranged on the tree.

"What are those?"

"Long-nosed bats!"

Bats on a sunlit tree? I couldn't help but shiver, a mix of rain chill and unexpected sights. My camera was snug in its bag, but my mind snapped pictures, capturing the moment vividly.

With rain persisting, the kayak carried us along the yellow river, birds occasionally darting overhead. All other critters sought shelter, leaving us thoroughly soaked. This might not have been the plan, but it sure had a flavor of its own—a playful twist. Just like that bird at breakfast, braving the rain seemed like another whimsical act in the grand play of life. And you know what? Rafting in the rain? Totally worth it for the unique experience it brought!

assistants steadied the kayak, and one by one, we hopped on board. With a firm push, we glided along, not fighting the rapids, but peacefully drifting downstream.

"Why's the river so murky? Is it always like this?" I asked, curious.

"Recent heavy rainfall stirred up the sand and gravel beneath the river. Usually, it's a deep green, but you know, climate's been acting up lately. Global warming's no joke!" the leader explained as we paddled leisurely.

As the rain picked up, I stashed my camera in a dry bag. As we drifted towards the shore, the leader and assistant worked hard to steer us backward until we gently bumped against a tree trunk. The leader then pointed out the tiny black spots dotting a tall tree and asked:

"See those small black spots? Any guesses what they might be?"

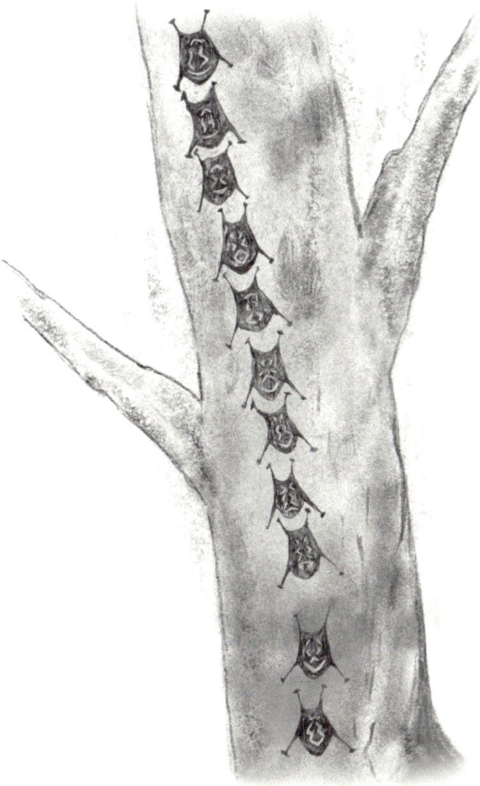

long-nosed bats on the tree trunk

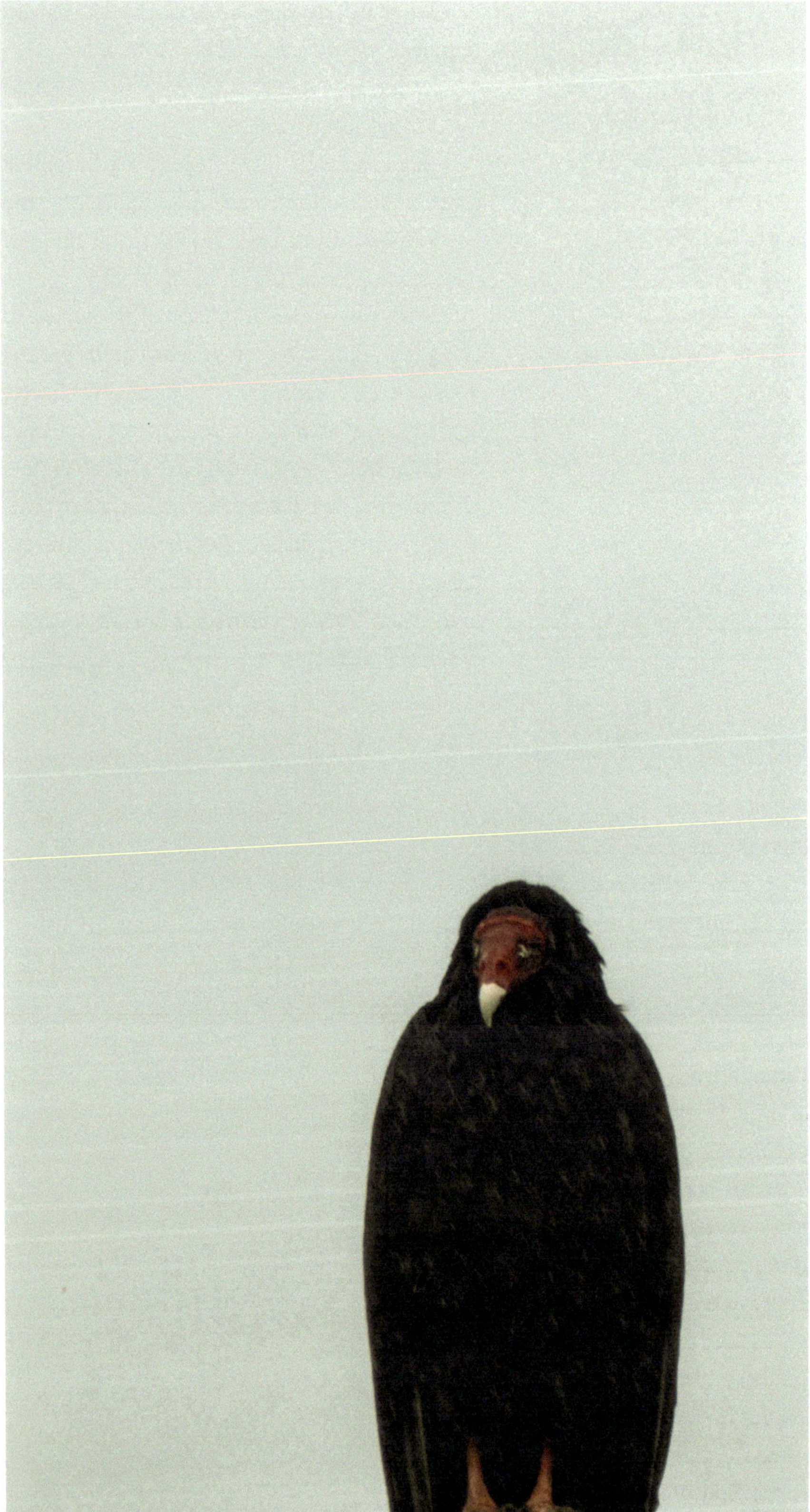

Beneath the Volcano

Attire in Black with Crimson Countenance

Here I am in La Fortuna, where the landscape is dominated by not one, but two imposing volcanoes: Arenal and Cerro Chato. Now, tackling Cerro Chato might sound like a big feat—it takes a good four hours and isn't exactly a walk in the park. But fear not, because Arenal has a couple of trails that'll scratch that hiking itch without leaving you feeling like you've just wrestled a mountain.

Today, I decided to lace up my boots and hit the Arenal Volcano Hike. And let me tell you, it's a breeze compared to its cousin, Cerro Chato. This trail is like a well-paved highway through the wilderness. No dirt paths to stumble over or steep hills to climb—just a smooth, flat path surrounded by towering trees swaying in the breeze.

But of course, no adventure is complete without a few surprises, right? Just when I was getting into my stride, I found myself in the midst of a mosquito convention. These little buggers were buzzing around me like I owed them money, leaving itchy reminders all over. Thank goodness for mosquito repellent with the powerful chemical DEET, even if it does smell like something out of a chemistry lab. It might make me feel like I'm wearing a hazmat suit, but hey, anything to keep those bloodsuckers at bay.

Here's the scene: I'm strolling out of the woods, just taking in the scenery, when I stumble upon this adorable little stone house with a roof that could have been plucked straight out of a fairytale. But here's where things get interesting—perched on top are these two birds that look like they're straight out of a mystery novel.

I'm talking big birds, decked out in black feathers and sporting these striking red faces. But here's the kicker—they've got eyes that seem to have a mind of their own, nostrils right smack in the middle of their faces, and these sharp white beaks that make them look like they mean business. And don't even get me started on their wings—they're draped over their bodies like they're wearing fancy black coats. Oh, and did I mention their feet? Red and gray, with claws that could probably give Wolverine a run for his money.

Now, add a little rain into the mix, and these birds suddenly transform into something straight out of a film noir. They're standing there, all aloof and mysterious, like they've got secrets to spare. I half expected them to start whispering about some grand scheme or plotting a devious plot.

But here's the twist: when you take a step back and look at them as a pair, they lose some of that sinister edge. Suddenly, they're not ruthless assassins or master manipulators—they're just a couple of lovebirds, although with a flair for the dramatic. It's funny how a change in perspective can turn even the most mysterious characters into nothing more than a quirky duo enjoying a rainy day together.

After shaking off the noir vibes, I kept on trekking until I reached the edge of Arenal Lake. Despite the gray skies and drizzle, there was something strangely beautiful about the scene. The lake mirrored the sky's moody tones, and the rustling leaves added a touch of magic to the air. No matter if the sun's shining bright or the clouds are painting the sky gray, there's something special about each day for those who know how to find the magic in it.

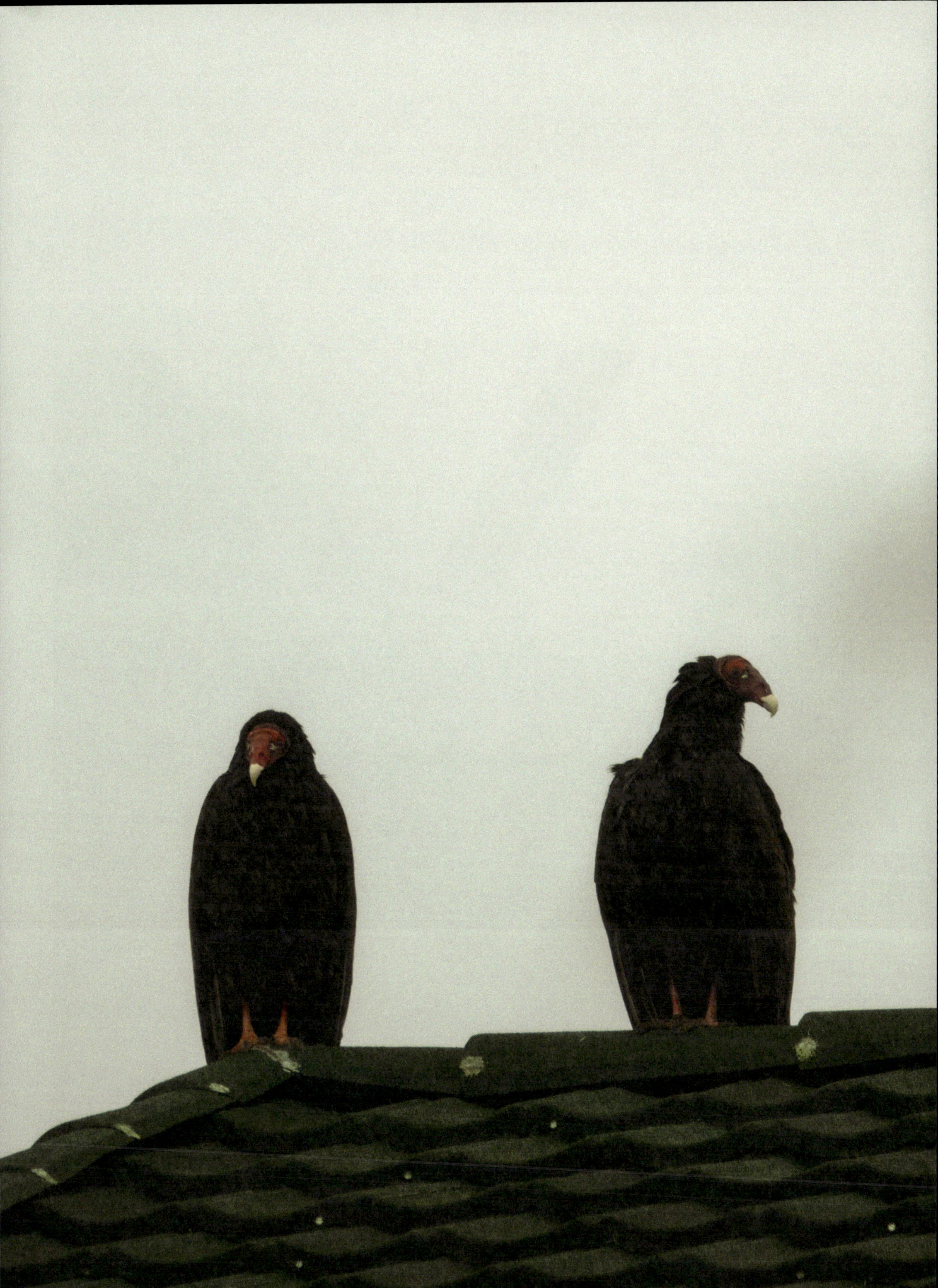

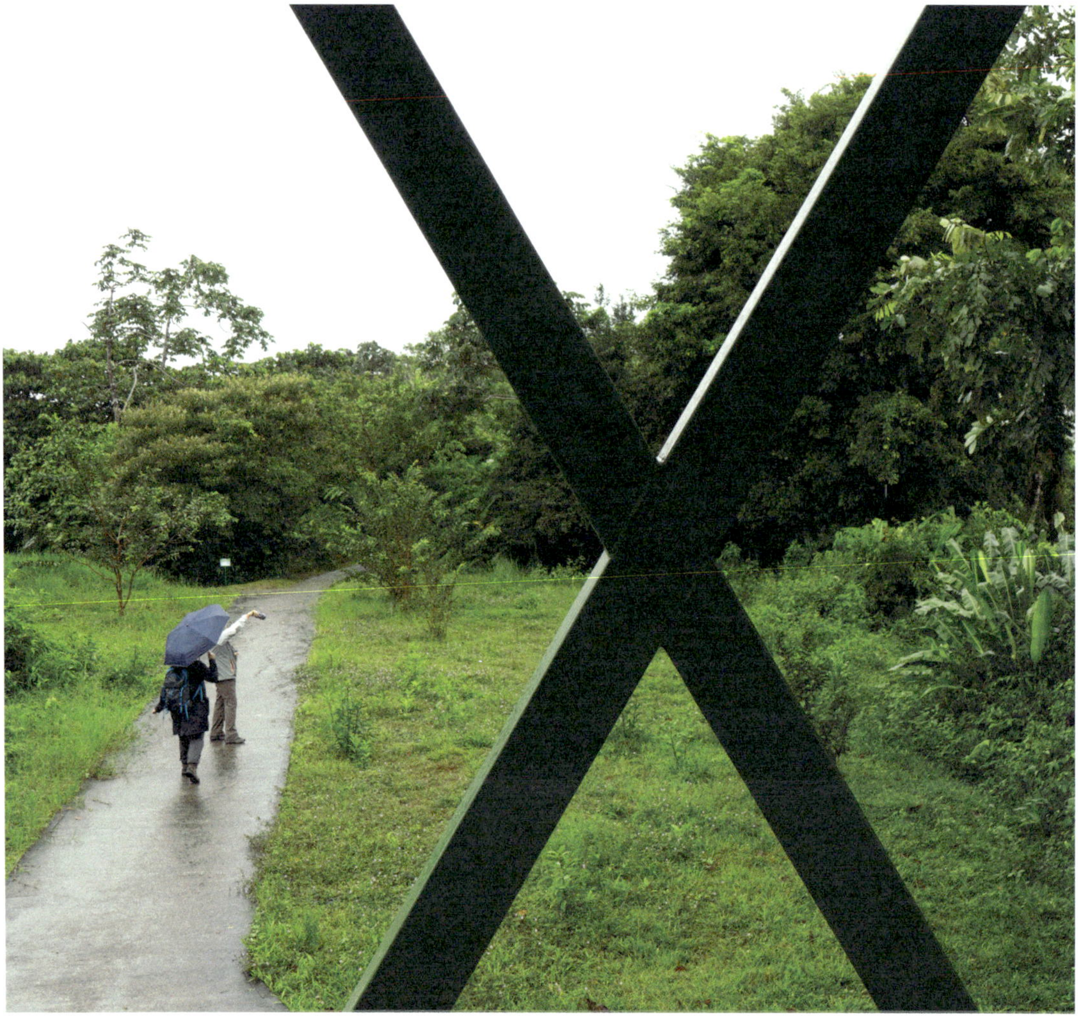

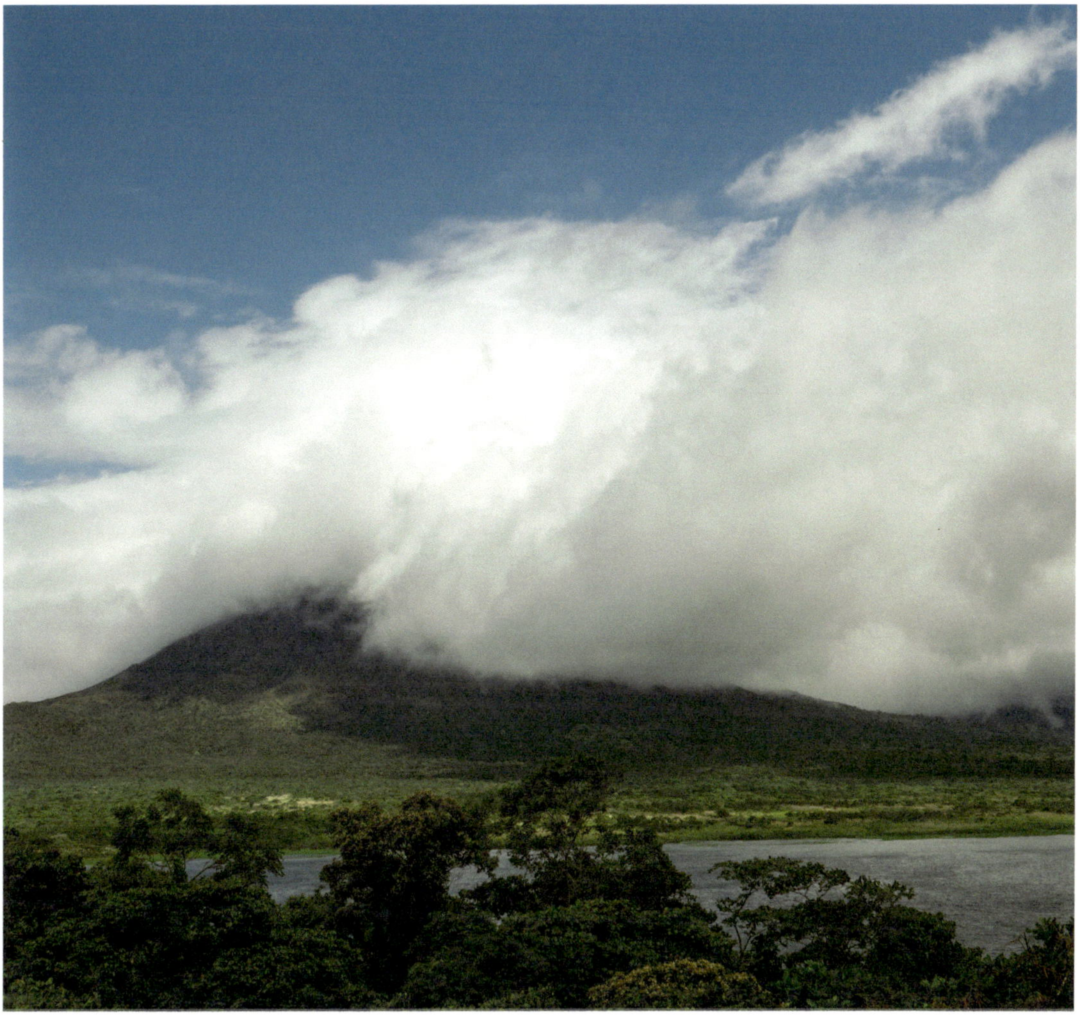

La Fortuna

2 hr 54 min / 116 km

Monteverde

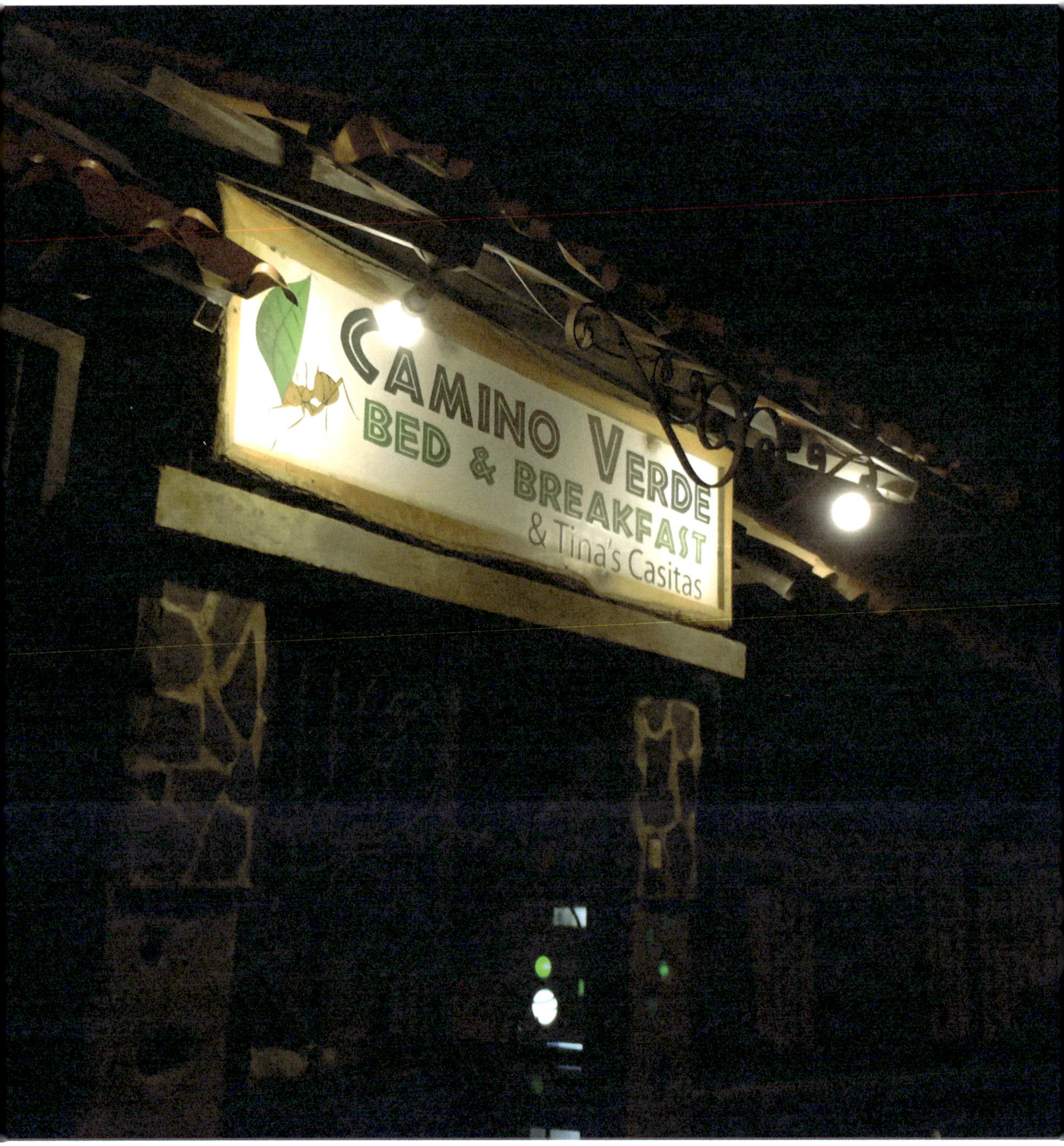
CAMINO VERDE
BED & BREAKFAST
& Tina's Casitas

Nightclub Takeout in a Small Town

I hopped into the Dai-fat-zai, ready to leave La Fortuna behind and head for Monteverde—a 149-kilometer adventure that promised about three hours of twists and turns. Now, I must say, a good chunk of that journey was on a dirt road straight out of an off-road rally. Potholes? Oh, you betcha! They were like little surprises waiting to jolt me out of my seat.

But fear not, because I fancied myself quite the road warrior, smoothly switching the Dai-fat-zai from two-wheel drive to four-wheel drive like a pro. Yet, try as I might, those pesky potholes were relentless. Every bump had me holding onto the edge of my seat, wondering if we'd lose a tire along the way. But you know what? The Dai-fat-zai held its own, bouncing back each time like a champ, ready to tackle whatever lay ahead.

Let me paint you a picture of Monteverde—it's not your run-of-the-mill town; oh no, it's more like a patchwork quilt of cozy little communities. Forget fancy pants five-star hotels; here, it's all about those charming little spots that have character bursting at the seams. And lucky me, I snagged a spot at the Camino Verde Bed & Breakfast in the quaint town of Santa Elena.

As I rolled up in the Dai-fat-zai, the road was sandy and muddy, kicking up a storm of dust behind me that made me feel like I was in the middle of a desert escapade. The parking lot at the hotel was already chock-full, so I ended up squeezing into a spot on the roadside. Stepping out, I was met by a strong gust of wind that seemed to declare, "Welcome to paradise."

Pushing open the creaky door of the hotel, I stepped into a whole new world. The reception area was cozy as can be, with a young dude chilling on a worn-out sofa, lost in the depths of the internet. Next to him, a freezer stocked with all sorts of drinks caught my eye, promising refreshment in the tropical heat.

But it was the scene beyond the reception desk that really caught my attention. Check this out: two girls deep in gossip over coffee, a dude engrossed in a book but sneakily peeking at a silent TV, and a family quietly duking it out in a game of poker. And just beyond them, an open kitchen beckoned, with all the fixings for a cozy cup of tea or coffee.

And oh, don't even get me started on the view! Through a glass door, a small platform offered a peek at the lush green forest beyond, like something straight out of a fairy tale. Yep, Monteverde was shaping up to be one heck of an adventure.

"Hey there! What can I do for you?" came a friendly voice from behind the desk. I turned around to see a young guy with a big grin plastered on his face.

"Hi, I've got a room reservation here," I replied with a smile of my own.

"Welcome!" he said cheerfully, tapping away at the computer to confirm my booking. After a bit of clicking and clacking, he handed me a printed paper along with the key.

"So, your room's just through the glass door, turn left onto the platform. Here's a map with all the cool stuff around town. Also, breakfast is included and served at 6:30 in the morning. It's made fresh, so give us a bit of time. Help yourself to coffee or tea—it's right there. Plus, feel free to use any tableware; just tidy up afterward. Oh, and about those drinks in the fridge, they're not complimentary. If you fancy one, just make sure to settle the tab the next day if there's no one around at night. Got all that?" he rattled off in one breath.

The whole 'pay later' thing caught me off guard. In the city, you'd expect everything to be locked down tight or replaced with those pesky vending machines.

"Got it. Say, are you from around here? How long have you been running the show?" I asked, curious about the guy behind the desk.

"Yeah, born and raised! My old man owns this place, and me and my brothers keep things ticking. It gets pretty busy, but we manage just fine," he replied with a hint of pride in his voice.

"No wonder this place feels so cozy. It's got that homey vibe, not your typical hotel feel," I remarked, impressed by the familial touch.

"Thanks! We try to make everyone feel at home here," he said with a grin.

With the key in my pocket and my bags in tow, I stepped onto the platform, feeling the wind's playful tug. Making a left turn, I spotted another cabin with an inviting round arch. Its walls, crafted from glass bottles with a whimsical polka dot pattern, added a touch of charm to the scene. Despite its cozy size, the room felt fresh and tidy, dispelling any hint of nostalgia.

After a quick breather, my stomach grumbled, signaling it was time to hunt down some grub. Upon returning to the hotel, I found myself lingering, not quite ready to call it a night. With the clock striking nine, I decided to venture out and explore the nightlife of this charming little town.

In the midst of a light drizzle, a nearby bar beckoned to me. Stepping inside, I found only a handful of patrons—a couple engaged in lively conversation with the bartender, their Spanish banter a mystery to my ears. The man's booming voice and the woman's infectious laughter painted a picture of merriment. Taking a seat at the bar, I caught the bartender's eye, hoping to join in on the fun.

"So, what's your poison?" she asked in flawless English, a hint of mischief in her eyes.

"Hmm, what's the crowd favorite?" I queried, scanning the shelves behind her.

"Beer or liquor, my friend. No fancy cocktails here! If you're into beer, you can't go wrong with Imperial. It's the go-to for everyone in Costa Rica!" she exclaimed, already reaching for a frosty bottle.

"Only bottled though, right? No draft?" I inquired, hoping for a frothy pint.

"Yep, bottles only. But trust me, it's the best you'll ever taste!" she assured me, a confident grin on her face.

Just then, the boisterous guy at the end of the bar raised his Imperial triumphantly. "Cheers to that! This stuff's as good as your Tsingtao beer!" he declared, his voice echoing through the cozy bar.

"Alright then, I'll take one! By the way, do you guys ever sip on Tsingtao?" I asked, curious to hear their take on Chinese brews.

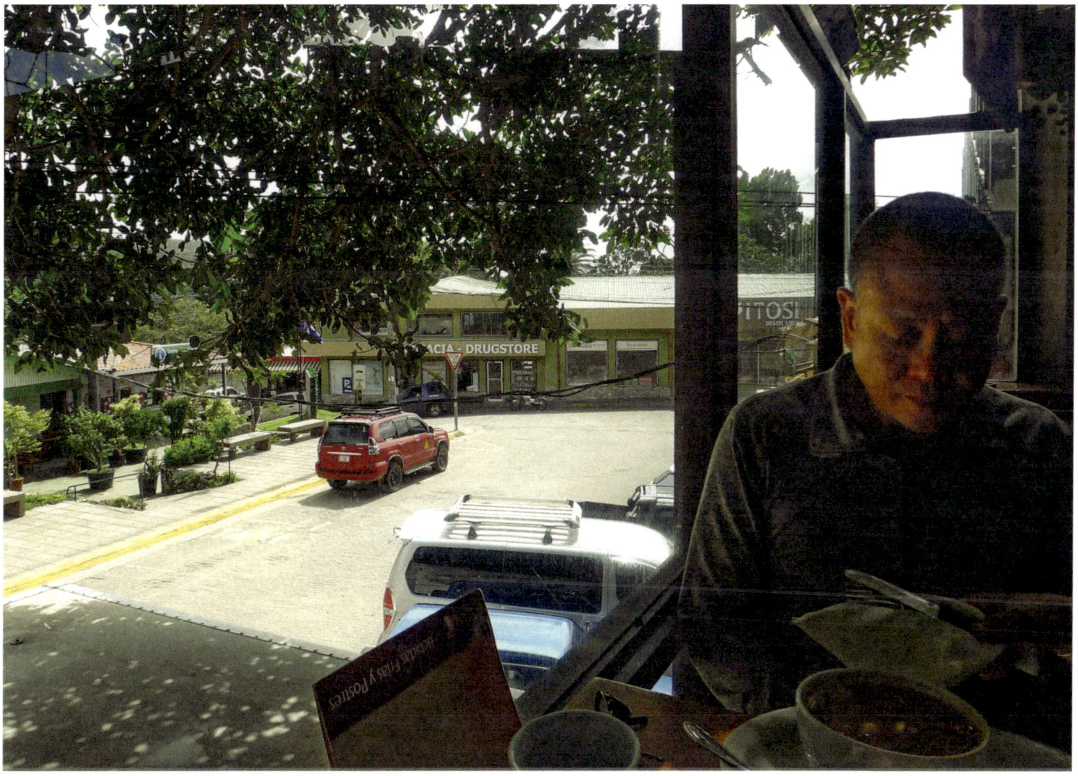

Enjoying lunch break at the small town.

"I've traveled far and wide, my friend—China, Europe, Ireland—but nothing beats the local brew here. Imperial's in a league of its own," he replied, a sense of hometown pride evident in his words.

You know, it's a scene you'll find in bars all around the globe—locals proudly championing their hometown brew as the best thing since sliced bread. They've globe-trotted, tasted every tipple under the sun, and still come back swearing by the stuff brewed right at home. Whether it lives up to the hype or not, it's all about hometown pride.

It's like the way folks talk about their mom's cooking, right? That comfort food that no Michelin-starred chef could ever replicate. There's just something about that familiar taste that hits different. Believe it or not, getting into a beer debate with one of these locals is like stepping into a labyrinth—you might find yourself trapped in a discussion that could go on 'til the crack of dawn!

After shooting the breeze with the guy and gal, they bid adieu and headed out. I still had half a bottle of Imperial left when the bartender dropped the bombshell—the bar was closing up shop.

I glanced at my watch, puzzled. Ten minutes to ten? Seemed kinda early to call it a night. But as I looked around, I noticed only two other folks lingering, getting ready to call it quits.

With a shrug and a sigh, I chugged down the rest of my brew, feeling like I'd barely gotten started. Sometimes, you just gotta roll with the punches and make an early exit, even when you're not quite ready to.

Strolling aimlessly along the street, the wind now more of a gentle breeze, I felt at ease in the embrace of the night. Most of the shops and eateries had called it a day, their shutters down for the night. Before I knew it, I had wandered to the town's lone nightclub, its thumping beats beckoning from a distance.

As I approached, I couldn't help but notice a police car parked nearby, the officers chatting cordially with passersby—a reassuring sight that signaled a safe environment. Intrigued by the promise of a vibrant nightlife, I decided to check out the club. In fact, I'm not usually one for loud music, especially in nightclubs, but seeing the crowd moving in sync on the dance floor to let loose some pent-up energy—it felt like something out of an apocalyptic movie.

Entering the club's vicinity, a bouncer intercepted me, directing my attention to the nearby ticket booth. "Admission is $10," he declared.

Although the price seemed fair, my enthusiasm waned, prompting me to change my plans.

"Actually, I just fancy a beer. Any bars nearby?" I inquired instead.

"Only beer," the bouncer replied, exchanging a few words in Spanish with a nearby colleague before turning back to me. The other guy dashed off briefly before returning with two cans of beer.

"Two cans, $3 each, $6 total," the bouncer stated matter-of-factly.

I never would've guessed you could buy beer outside a club, let alone snagging the finest Imperial. Talk about unexpected surprises!

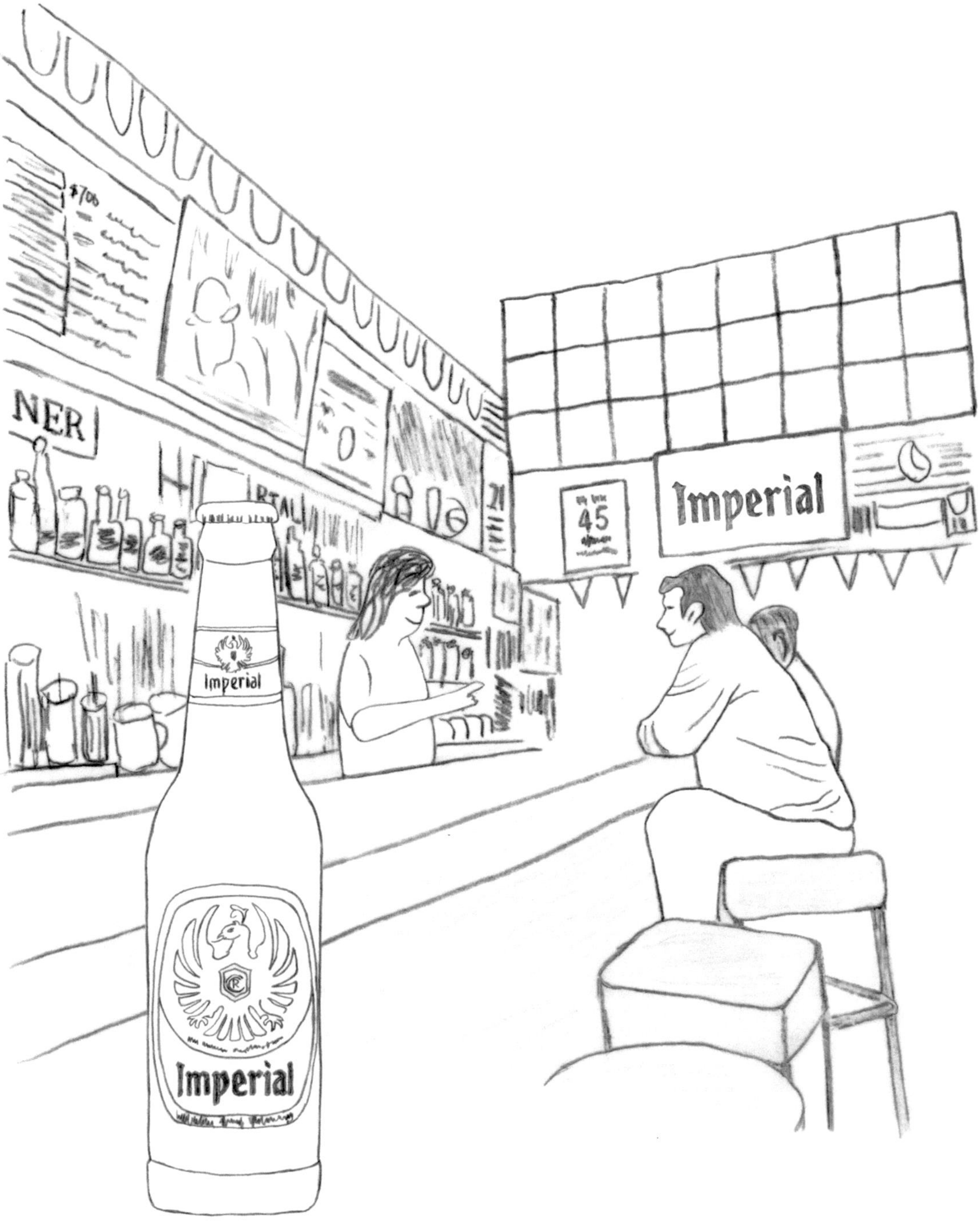
NER
Imperial
45
Imperial
Imperial

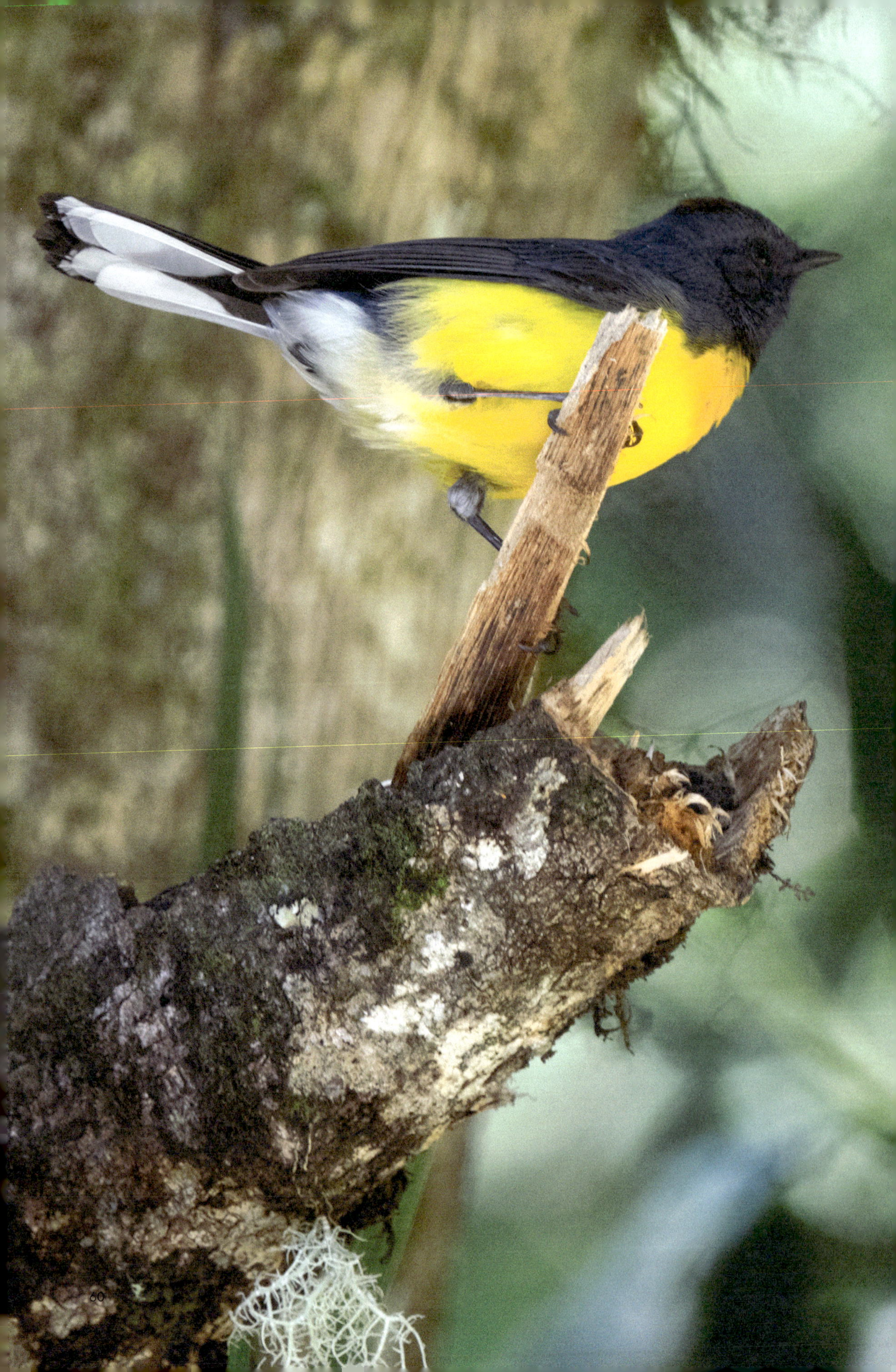

Free and Wild Salsa Dance

You know, it's been ages since I stepped foot in a zoo. Not my favorite thing, seeing animals stuck in cages and all. But hey, let's not get into that debate, especially not when we're talking about places dedicated to helping injured critters!

So, this time around, we weren't walking into your typical zoo. Nope, no lions, tigers, or elephants in sight. Instead, we found ourselves in a place where birds flitted about freely, no cages in sight!

Now, let me fill you in on this gem called the Monteverde Cloud Forest Reserve. It's been around since '72, covering a whopping 4,000 hectares of pure tropical cloud forest goodness. And get this, it's like a conservationist dream born from the efforts of the Quakers, the OG settlers of this county. They saw how delicate these forests are and took action.

Off we went, ready to explore the trails snaking through the mountains. Clear signs, easy paths—perfect for a leisurely stroll. I had my route all planned out until I heard these folks chatting near the ticket office:

"Find a guide who can dish out some history and help spot wildlife."

Wildlife spotting? Now that's my jam! But I gotta admit, I'm not usually one for tour guides. They tend to sound like they're reading straight from a textbook, which can be a snooze-fest. But hey, in a forest as dense as this, finding critters on your own could be a real challenge. So, I caved and decided to tag along with the guide.

Upon snagging my ticket, the attendant mentioned my tour guide was waiting outside. Stepping out, I spotted this guy not too far off, peering through a telescope like he's searching for hidden treasure. Naturally, I had to ask around:

"What's he looking at?"

"An eagle!"

"The eagle's hiding behind those branches. Get a peek, quick!" With that, the guy stepped back from the telescope.

Folks lined up politely, hoping for a glimpse of the majestic bird, but only the lucky few at the front got the show. Eventually, the eagle took off, and the crowd scattered. Just when I was about to go hunt down my guide, the telescope guy noticed my ticket and hollered:

"Hey, buddy, I'm your tour guide! Hang tight for a sec. We'll gather the gang and head off. We've got a two-and-a-half-hour journey ahead. Bathroom break now, if you need it!"

Ah, so he's the guide! Despite his stature, he had this quiet strength about him, with short hair and these bold eyebrows that could probably stop traffic. A bag of books hung from his waist, and he had all this gear slung around him like he's ready to conquer the jungle. And those arms? Clearly, he's no stranger to lifting heavy stuff.

After a short wait, six of us gathered up. You know, small group vibes always make for the best adventures. Once we got into the forest, our guide stopped us dead in our tracks.

"I'm Gabri, and you are..." We all exchanged names, and he made sure to remember each one.

"Ever wonder how many critters in this forest could ruin your day?"

Silence. We were all ears.

"Loads!"

A little startling, huh? But then he added:

"Don't sweat it though. Our hospitals have pretty much got you covered. There are a couple of sneaky snakes and spiders that even a helicopter couldn't save you from, but hey, no need to panic! Stick to the path, keep your hands to yourself, and you'll be golden. Any questions?"

We shook our heads, still processing.

"Alrighty then, let's roll!"

Gabri led the way, lugging his tripod like it weighed nothing. He paused for a moment, then dove into the backstory of the place, sharing tidbits about the tropical cloud forest and its inhabitants—birds, bugs, and beasts alike. Every now and then, he'd whip out his telescope, scan the area, then seamlessly slip back into conversation.

"Gabriel, you seem to know a ton about all the critters and plants here. Did you study this stuff in college?" I couldn't help but ask.

"Haha... College? Nah, never went!" He chuckled, pulling out a bunch of books from his waist bag, all about birds, bugs, and critters.

"These are my professors! I used to snap shots of animals and bugs, then spend my nights poring over books to learn more. Sometimes I'd hit up the library for extra info on this forest. Been reading for years now, and let me tell ya, mastering nature ain't no walk in the park!"

"Wow, that's some dedication!" chimed in a girl from up North.

"Hey, when you love something, laziness ain't

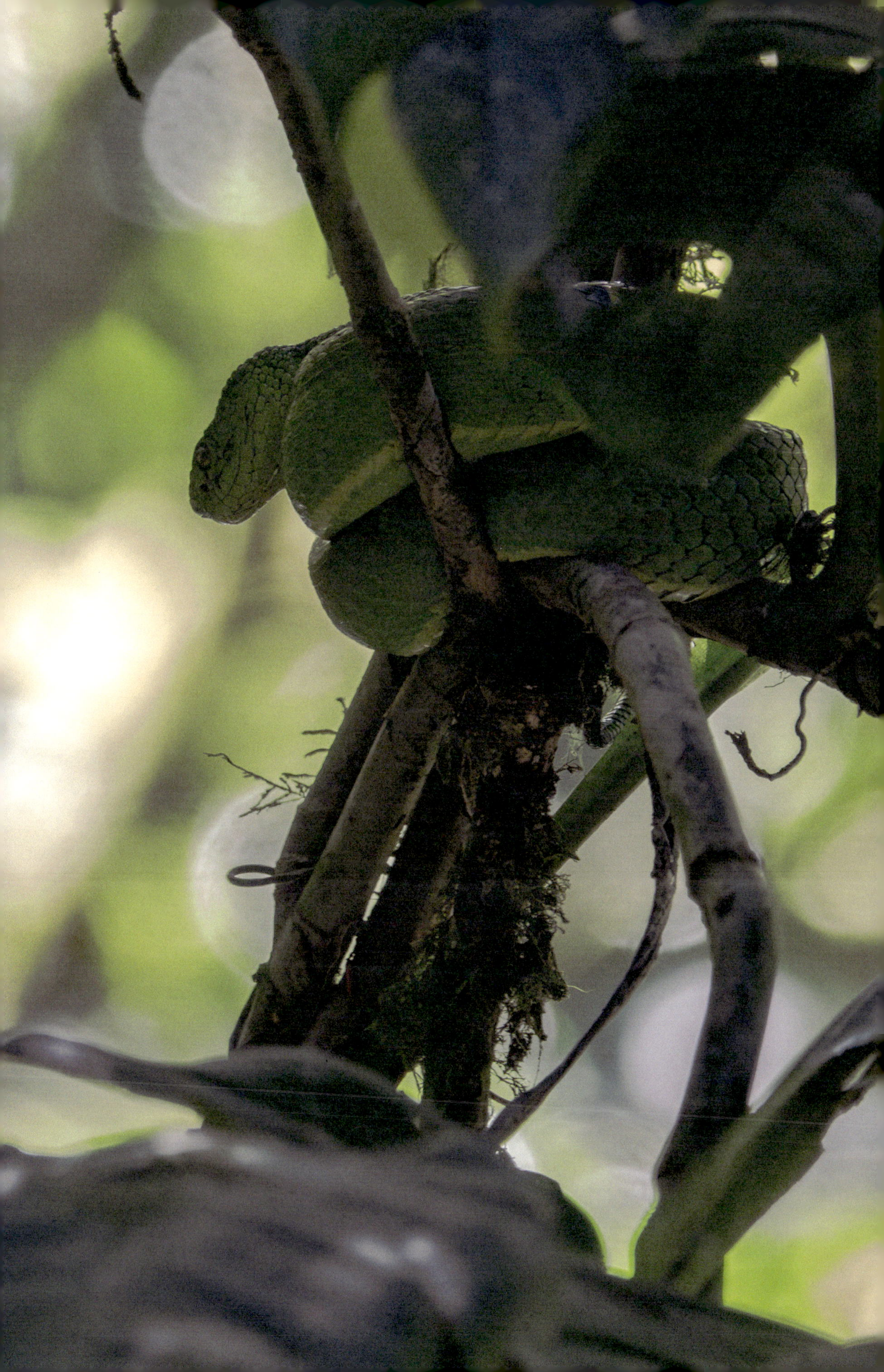

in the picture! I love this place, love what I do! Wandering these woods every day? It's the life!"

Just then, another guide showed up. After a quick chat, Gabri motioned for us to hurry along.

"Quick, let's move!"

We followed him around a bend in the trail, where he suddenly stopped and set up his tripod in a flash. Peering through his scope, he adjusted it and let out a gasp.

"Check it out... what a beaut!"

Perched up high in the trees, hidden amongst the leaves and branches, was this stunning bird. With a crown of blue-green feathers that looked like little cactus spines, sharp black eyes, and a bright yellow beak, it seemed almost shy, peeking out from behind the foliage. But its round body, decked out in a vibrant red vest and deep green coat, plus that elegant, flowing tail, made it look like it was dancing a spontaneous salsa right there on the branches! Before we could even applaud, it gracefully took off, reveling in its freedom.

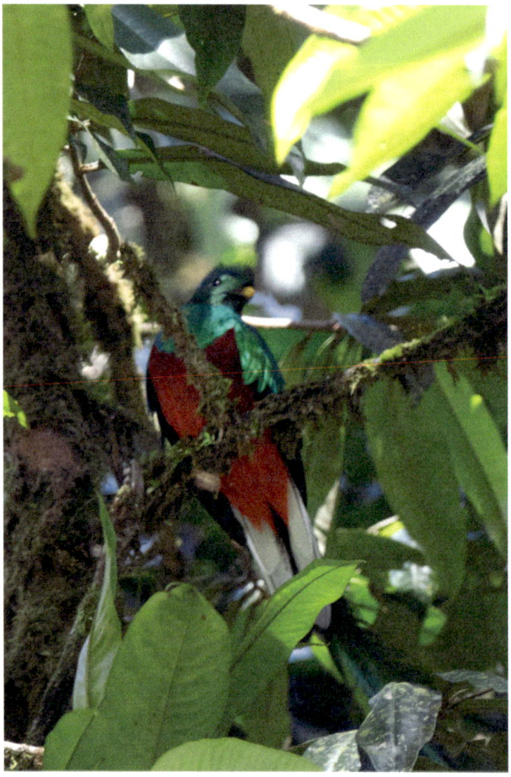

Once, I heard this story about a bird stuck in a cage. When it saw other birds flying free outside, it couldn't wrap its little bird brain around it. It was like, "Are they crazy? Just flapping around out there with no rhyme or reason!"

You see, that bird soaring through the sky? It's living the dream of freedom, feeling the wind beneath its wings. But the one stuck in the cage? It only gets a little taste of that freedom, stuck in its little bubble of safety. It's funny, though—lots of people choose that safety over the thrill of freedom, even though they've got every right to spread their wings and fly.

Monteverde Cloud Forest Reserve

https://cloudforestmonteverde.com/

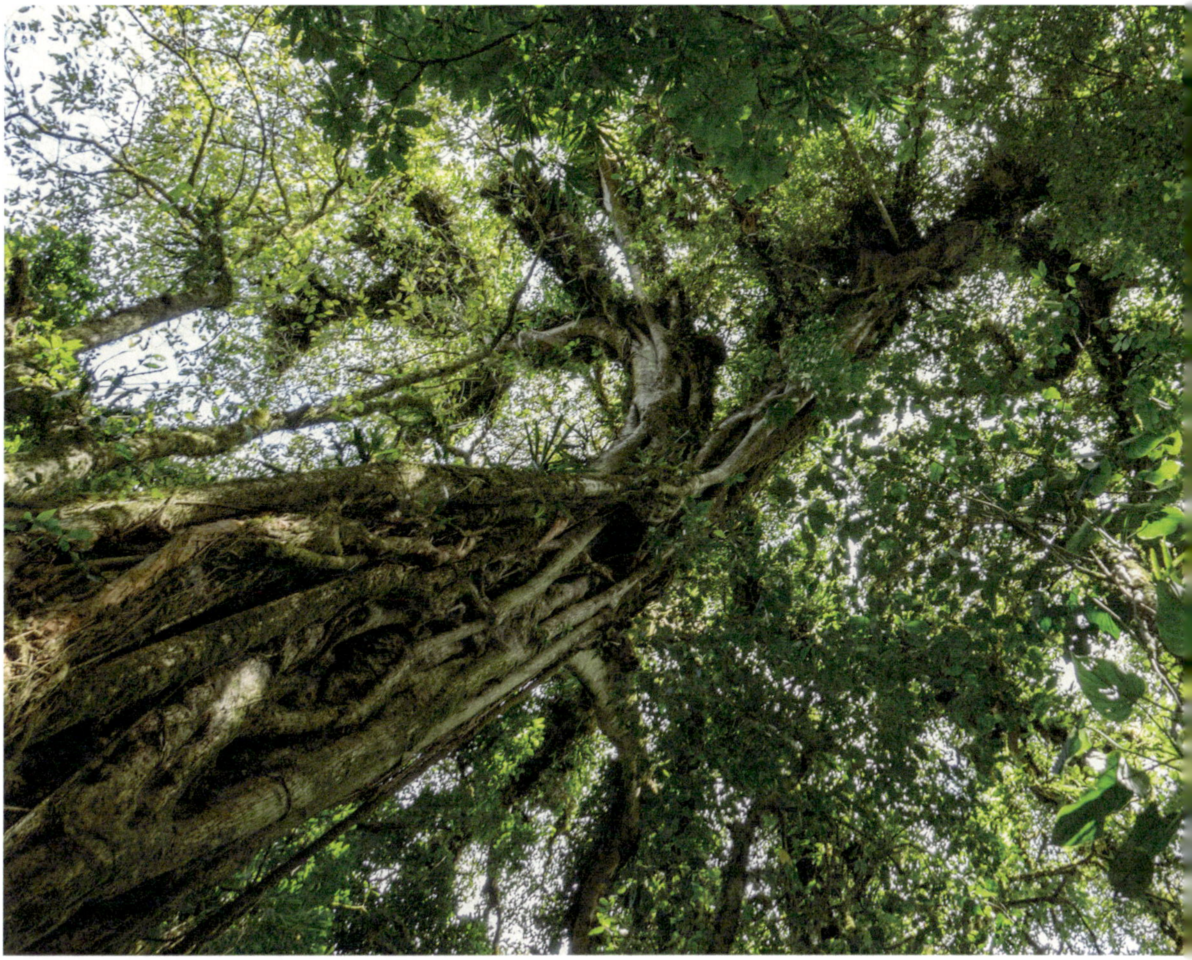

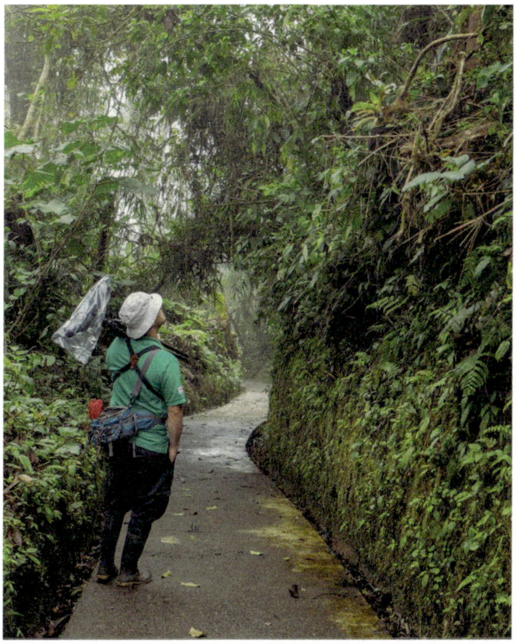

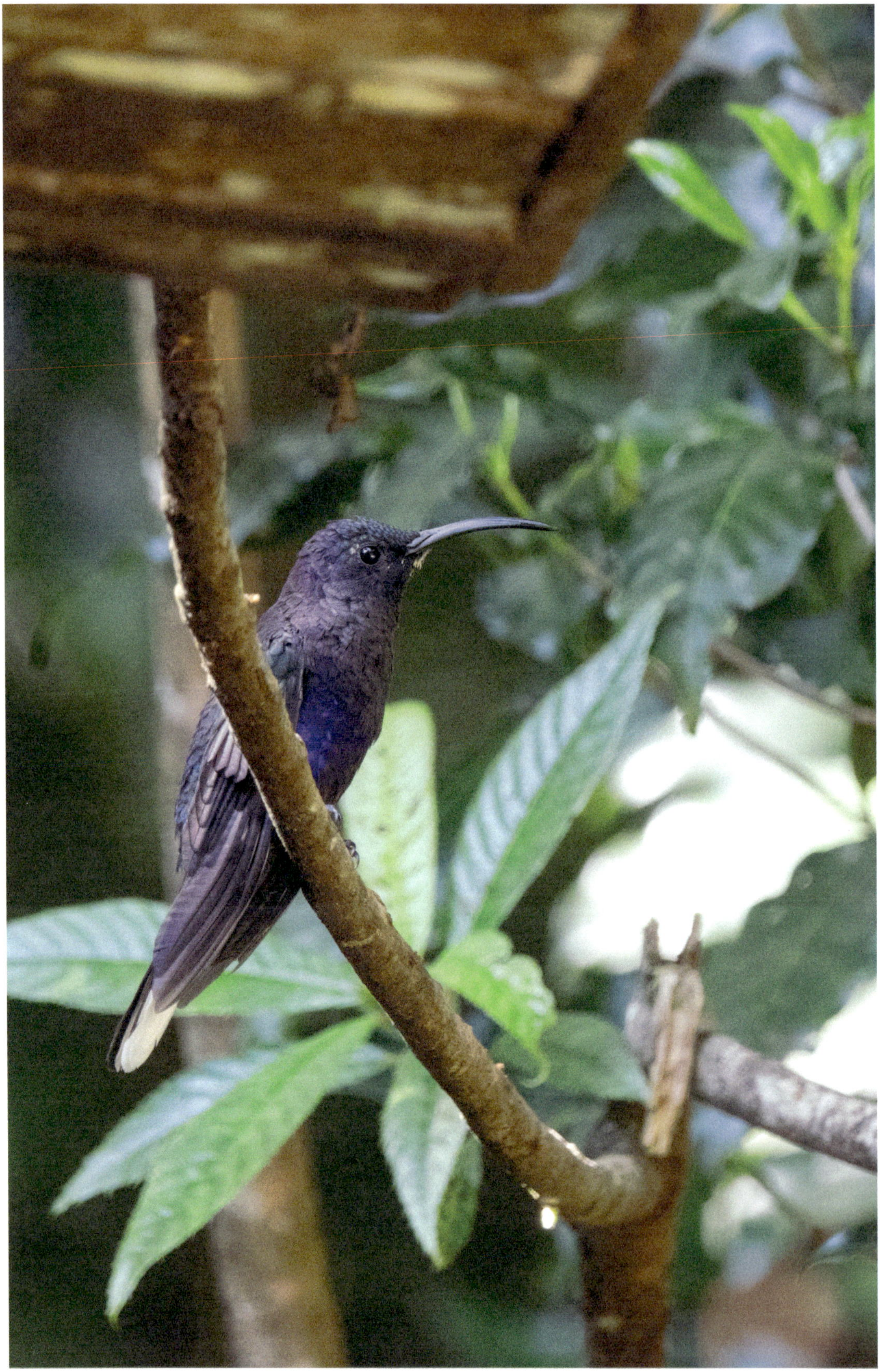

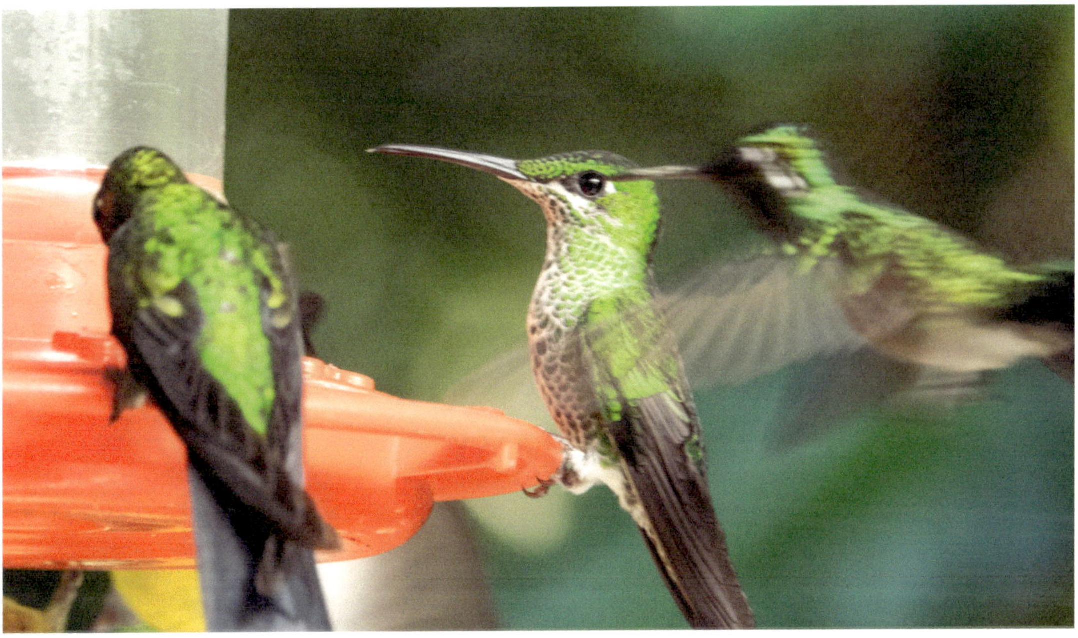

Wildlife

Costa Rica is a remarkable hub of biodiversity, hosting an astonishing variety of wildlife with over 500,000 species. This constitutes nearly 5% of the global total, ranking Costa Rica among the prestigious top 20 countries celebrated for their diverse ecosystems. Within this ecological wealth, insects make up a substantial portion, with over 300,000 species thriving in this natural treasure trove.

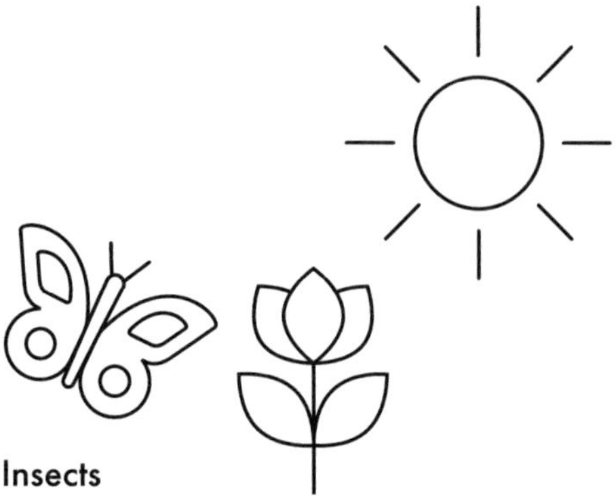

Insects

About 1,251 species of butterflies and at least 8,000 species of moths.

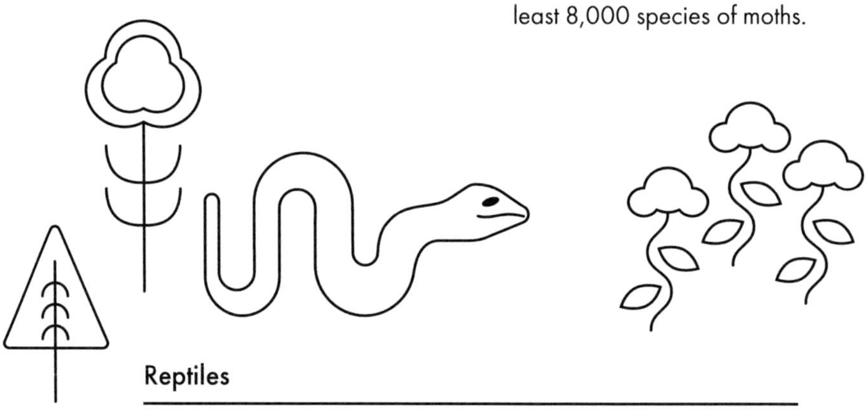

Reptiles

About 225 reptile species, including 70+ lizards and around 120 snakes, with roughly 20 being venomous.

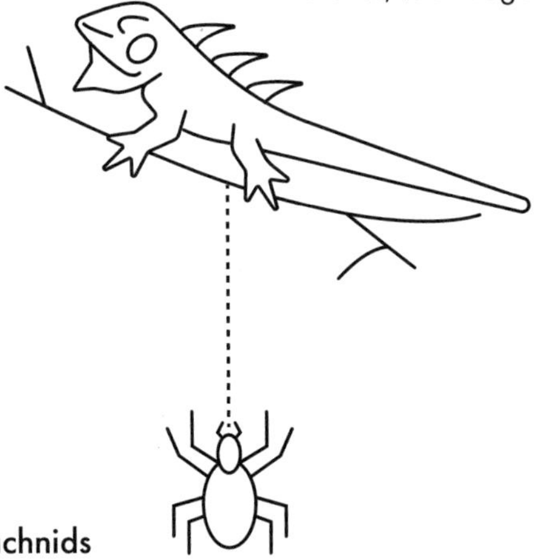

Arachnids

Nearly 2,000 spider species in the area, with tarantulas being the most common type found throughout.

The Ostional Wildlife Refuge

Established in 1984, safeguards millions of nesting turtles and permits legal egg harvesting to combat poaching.

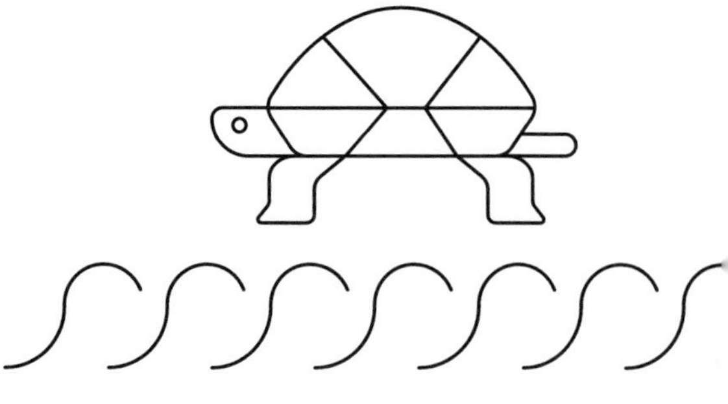

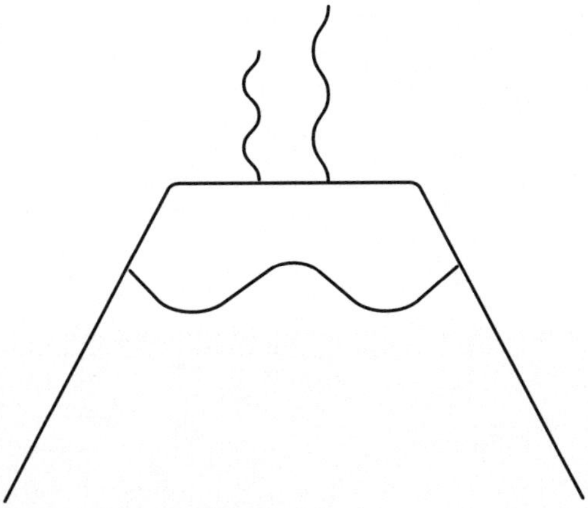

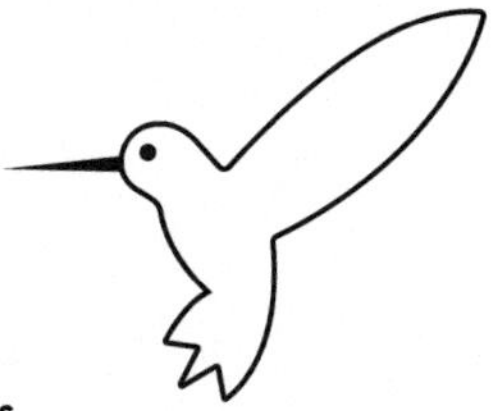

Birds

Among the 500,000 species, 900 are birds, including 52 hummingbird species.

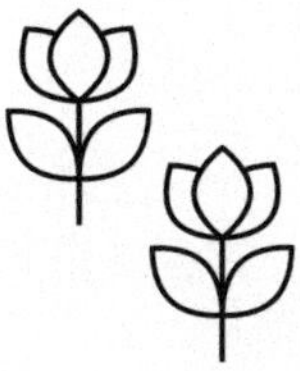

Volcanic formations

Over 200 volcanic formations, with about 100 showing activity and five currently active, some dating back 65 million years.

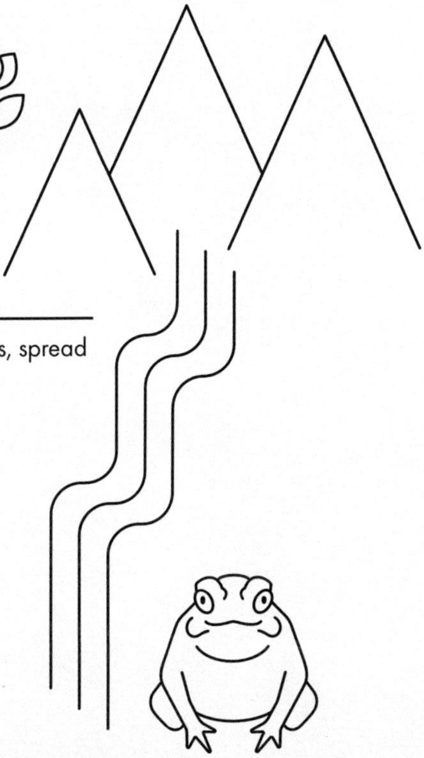

Waterfalls

More than 400 recorded waterfalls, spread all over the country.

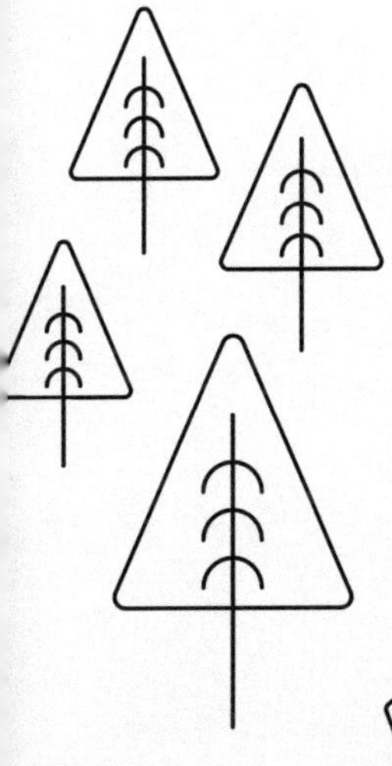

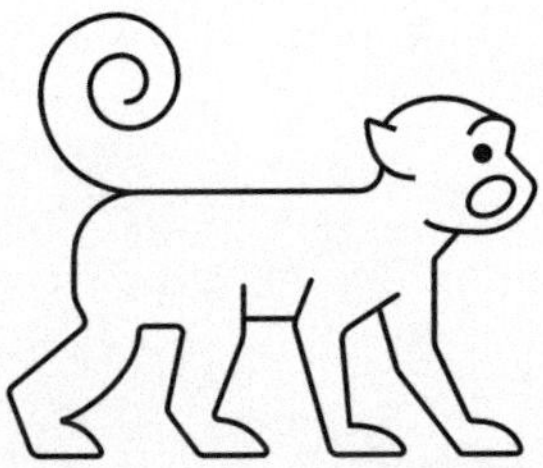

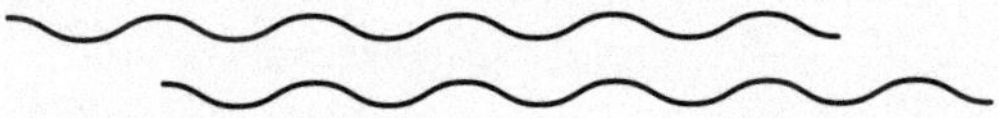

Mammals

There are nearly 250 mammal species, including four types of monkeys, such as the white-headed capuchin and mantled howlers, known for their lively behavior.

Amphibians

Approximately 175 amphibians inhabit this region, with frogs making up 85% of the total.

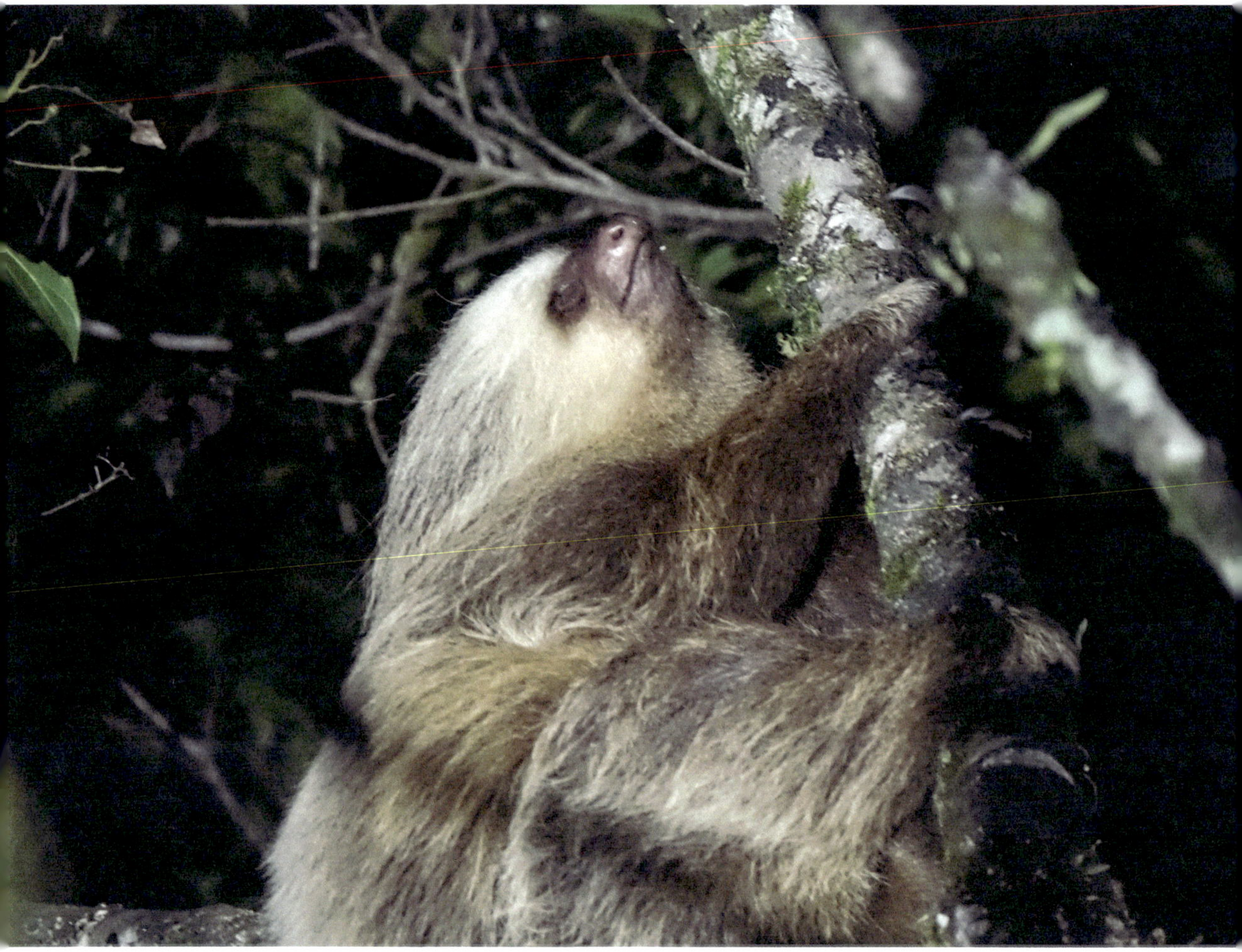

Life and Death in the Enigmatic Night

The wild, wild night, wrapped in a cloak of darkness so thick you could almost touch it. Every rustle in the bushes sets your heart racing, your mind conjuring up all sorts of mysterious creatures lurking just beyond your sight. But guess what? Amid all this eerie ambiance, Mother Nature's children are catching some Z's without a care in the world. Yep, while we're busy imagining monsters, the real stars of the show are snoozing away, totally unfazed by the spooky vibes. It's like a slumber party in the woods, and we're just lucky enough to be crashing it.

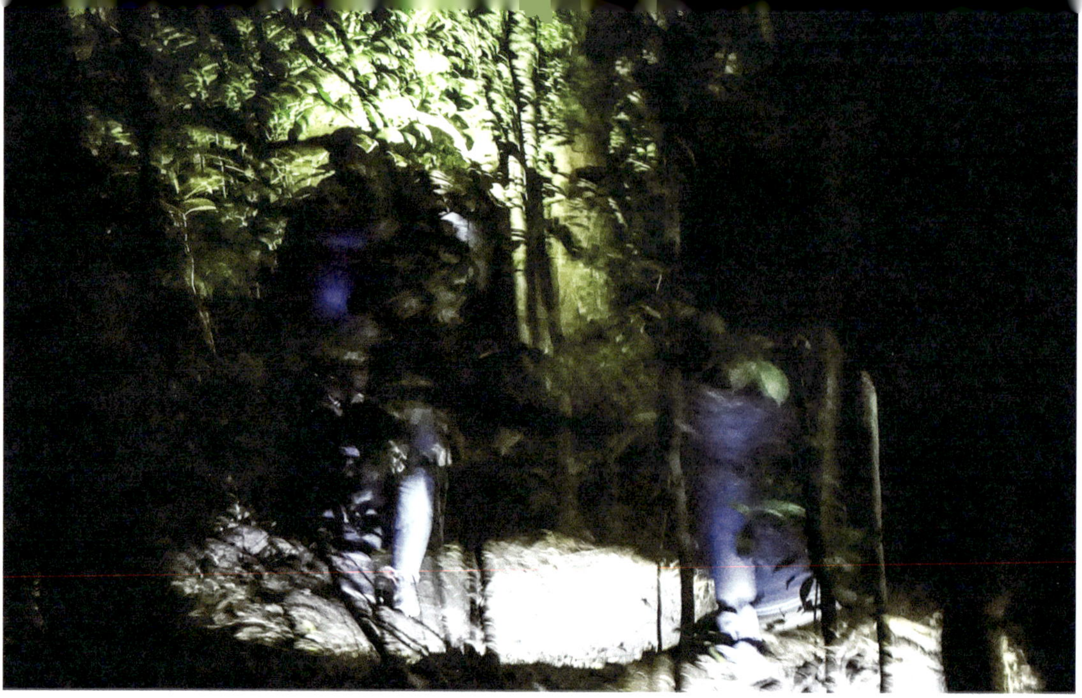

Venturing into the dark wilderness with only a flashlight, it felt like stepping into a dream—a surreal nighttime adventure.

So, here's the scoop: one night, I decided to spice things up and join the Kinkajou Night Walk. You know, a little after-dark adventure to see what the critters are up to while we're busy counting sheep. The tour guide and driver swooped in to pick me up from the hotel, and before I knew it, we were huddled in a cozy cabin on the edge of the forest, getting the lowdown on what to expect.

"Alright folks, before we dive into the wilderness, we've got a little paperwork to take care of," our guide announced, flashing us a grin like we're about to embark on the adventure of a lifetime.

"Just a quick sign-off to cover our tails in case anything wild happens – you know, like running into a snake with a chip on its shoulder or stumbling down a ravine. But don't sweat it, we've never had any fatalities from snake bites... yet!"

With a nervous chuckle, we each grabbed a waiver and pen, exchanging glances like we're all in this crazy expedition together. After a few scribbles and nods of reassurance, we were officially cleared for takeoff.

"Okay, now that we've got the legal stuff out of the way, let's talk flashlights," the guide continued, handing out beams of light like they're golden tickets. "These babies are your trusty sidekicks for the night. Just remember, keep 'em pointed down and your voices down too – we don't want to wake the critters! Stick close, follow my lead, and get ready for some serious excitement. Trust me, you're in for a wild ride!"

And off we went, plunging into the heart of the forest with a mix of excitement and trepidation. The towering trees swallowed up the starry sky, leaving us to rely on the feeble glow of our flashlights to navigate through the darkness. It was like wandering through a dream – everything around us cloaked in shadows, with only the occasional rustle of leaves to break the silence. I stuck close to the folks ahead of me, not wanting to get lost in this dark maze.

And then, there it was: our first snoozing superstar of the night, the two-toed sloth. Hanging upside down like it was the most natural thing in the world, with a lazy grin plastered across its face. Its fur shimmered in the dim light, reminding me of something out of a fairy tale. Sloths, man, they're the epitome of chill – lounging on a branch for days on end, only moving when absolutely necessary. I couldn't help but chuckle at the thought of them, like commuters in the morning rush hour, barely awake and clinging to anything for support. But hey, at least sloths get to clock in a solid fifteen hours of shut-eye every day, right?

"Can you believe it? We just stumbled upon the very spot where Xiaoqing used to chill – yeah, from that ancient Chinese legend about the White Snake!" I couldn't help but laugh at the coincidence, feeling like we've been dropped right into the pages of a modern-day fairy tale.

As I gazed upon the hefty, slow-moving green snake, the image of Xiaoqing's transformation flashed through my mind. In the story, she's all about that undercover life, masquerading as a drop-dead gorgeous human while hiding her true reptilian form. You know what, this snake wasn't exactly winning any beauty contests – but hey, who am I to judge?

With its twisted body coiled around the tree trunk like a circus act gone wrong, I couldn't help but find it strangely amusing. But don't let its clownish antics fool you; those pale gray eyes had a serious air about them, adding a dash of mystery to the whole scene. And thank goodness it was out like a light, sparing us from any impromptu snake charades.

As we approached the river's edge, we hit pause on our trek. The sound of flowing water cut through the stillness of the night with such clarity it was almost surreal. I aimed my flashlight into the water, and suddenly, the river transformed into this magical underwater world, shimmering with tiny fish and microorganisms.

"Alright, folks, let's try our luck! I've got a little surprise in store," our guide announced with a mischievous grin. He dashed to the other side of the river, plucked a leaf, and returned, motioning for us to gather around. Being stuck at the

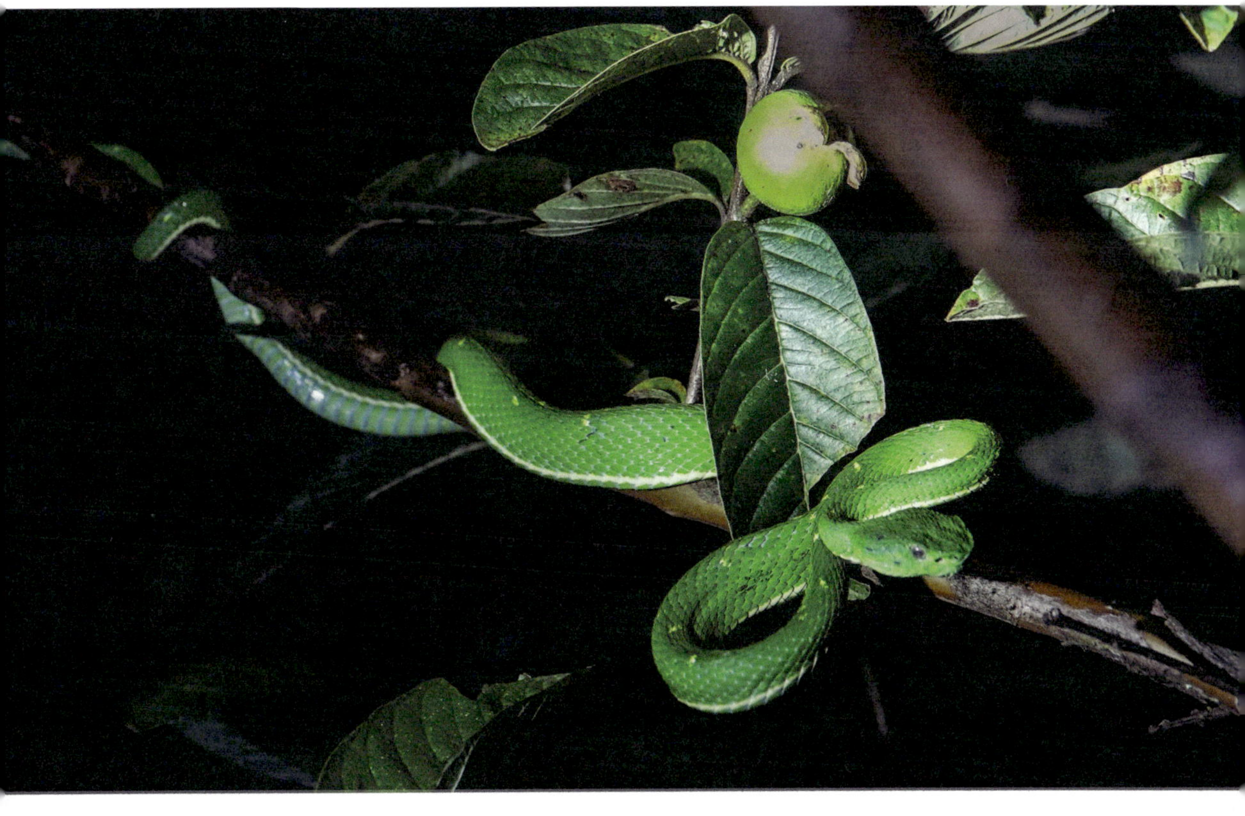

back, I couldn't quite see what was happening, but the guide urged those in front to make way so everyone could get a peek. Finally, it was my turn, and what a sight greeted me!

There, perched on a leaf, was the cutest little creature – a gaudy leaf frog, also known as the red-eyed leaf frog! Despite seeing it in souvenir shops before, I never realized just how tiny it was. Its crimson eyes seemed to glow against the night, giving it an almost otherworldly charm.

Now, here's the kicker: this little guy might look harmless, but it's got some serious survival skills. By day, it's a master of disguise, blending seamlessly with its surroundings. But when danger lurks, those fiery eyes come out to play, scaring off predators before making a swift getaway. Talk about a cool trick!

Those couple of hours in the dark woods flew by in the blink of an eye. Surprisingly, the critters of the night were nothing like the scary beasts you hear about in stories – they were just catching some Z's like the rest of us. A gentle breeze whispered through the trees, promising a peaceful night's sleep.

You know how it is in the city, surrounded by the warm glow of streetlights and the soft embrace of our beds. But for some of us, the idea of being out in the dark can be a bit spooky. It's easy to forget that our ancestors didn't have all the fancy stuff we've got now. It's like we've come to rely on all these modern luxuries just to get by.

But let's face it, all this reliance on technology and material things can't be good for the planet. We've gotta find a balance between enjoying our creature comforts and taking care of Mother Earth.

You know that old saying, "everything in moderation"? Well, turns out, it's onto something. Sure, we're all about our cozy beds and tech gadgets, but every now and then, we've gotta break free from the city grind. There's just something magical about escaping to nature, kicking back on a rock, and soaking in the moonlight. It's like all the stress and chaos just melt away, leaving nothing but peace and tranquility in their wake. Life's complicated enough as it is – sometimes, simplicity is exactly what we need to hit the reset button.

Kinkajou Night Walk

https://kinkajounightwalk.com

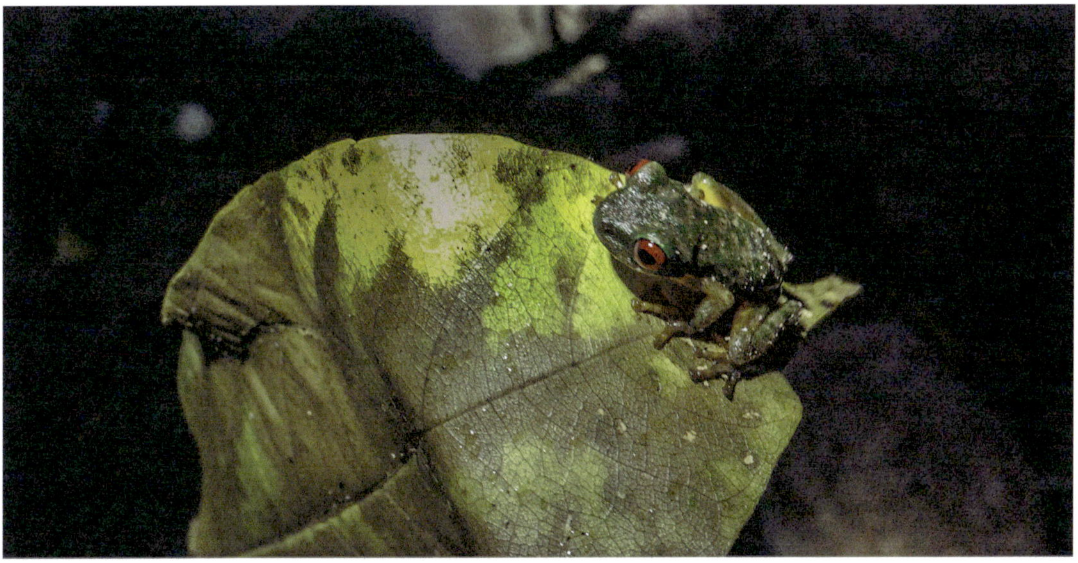

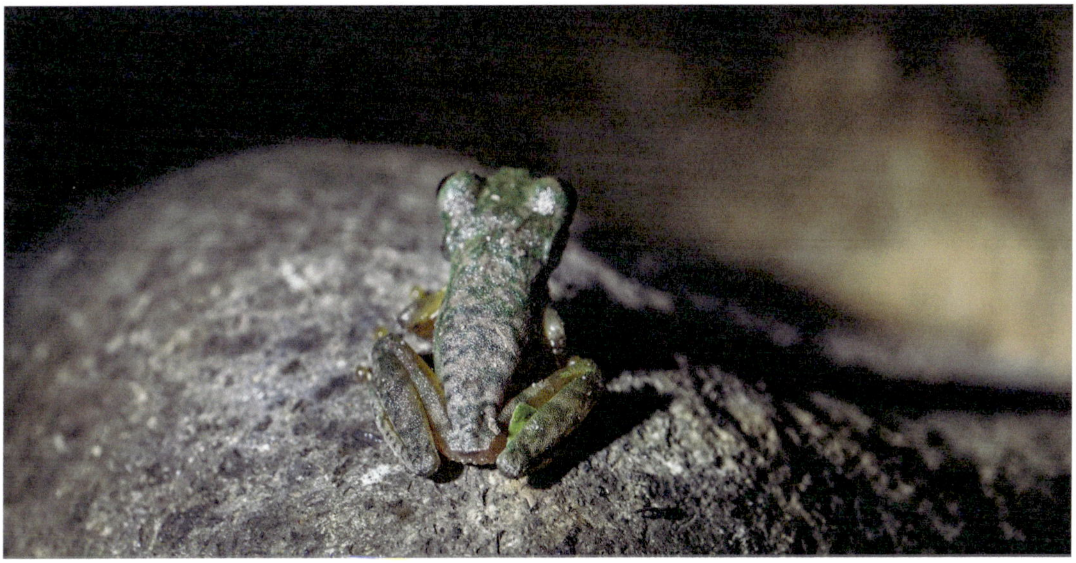

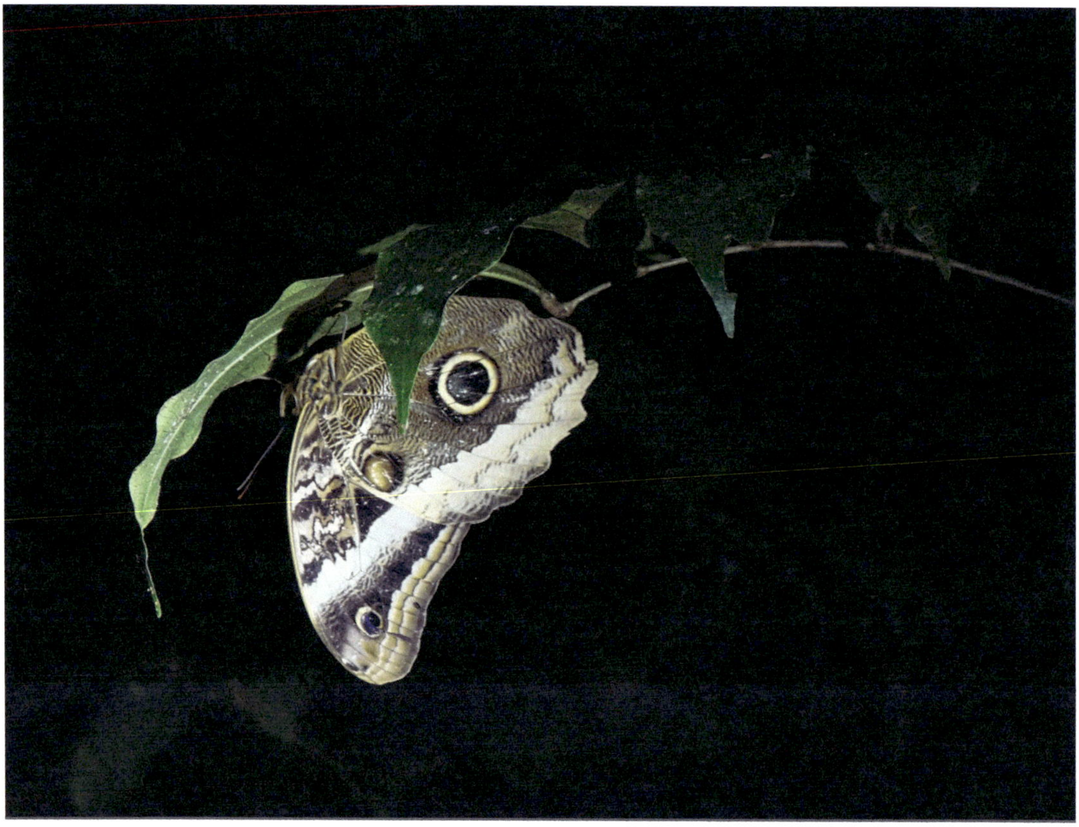

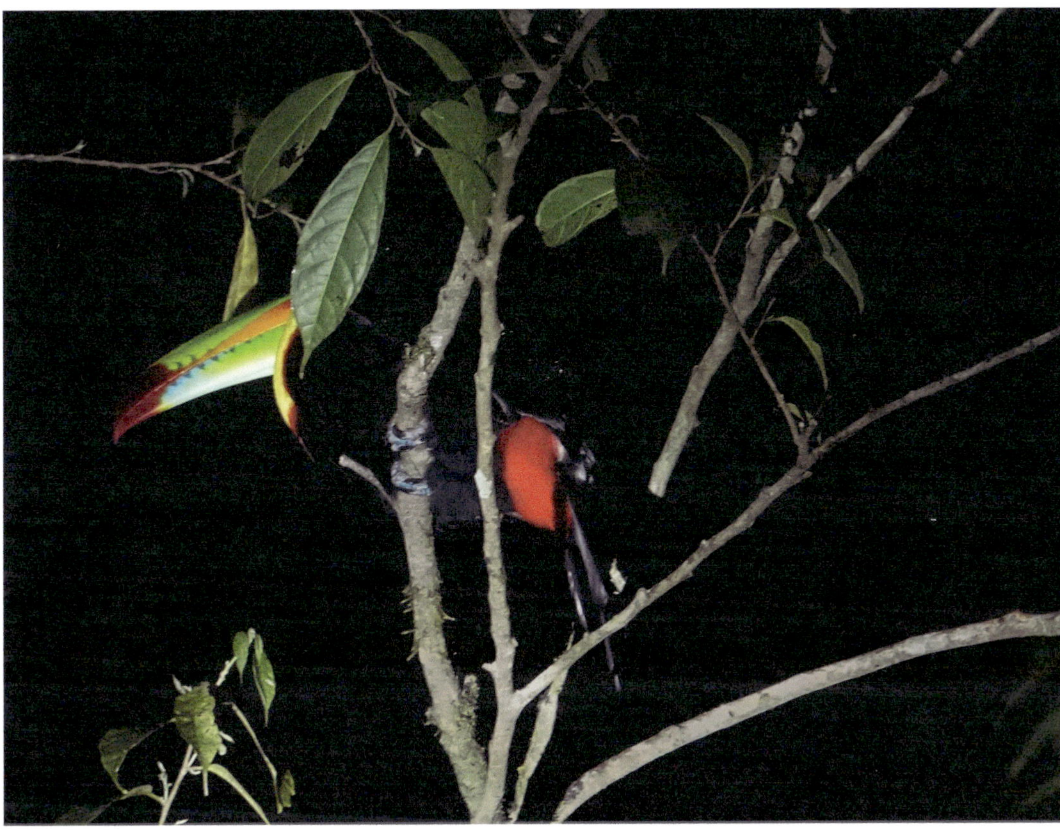

Monteverde

2 hr 12 min / 116 km

Llanos de Cortés

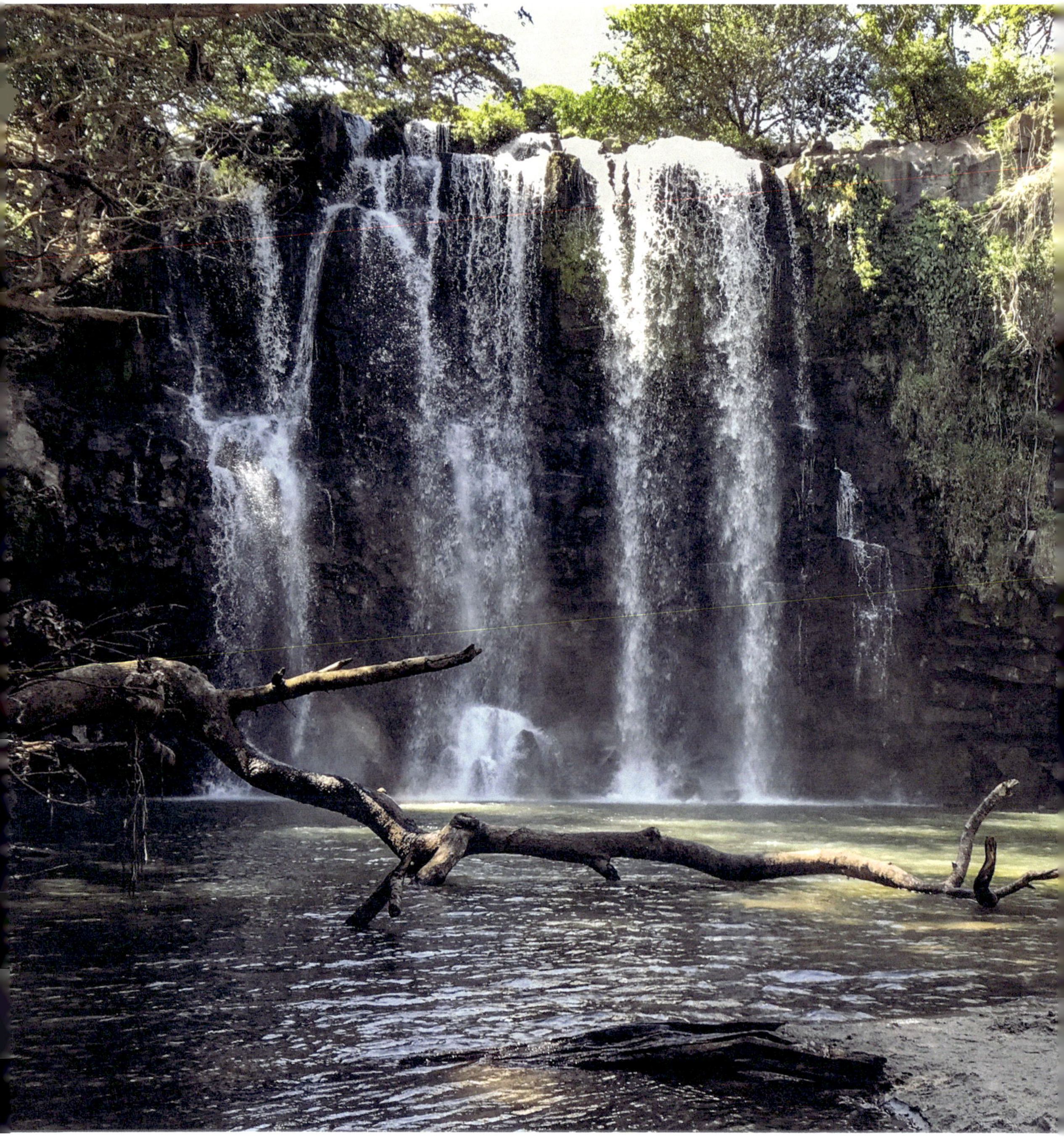

Behind the Waterfall

Time to kick this adventurous journey back into gear! After a scenic two-hour drive from Monteverde to Llanos de Cortes, we're greeted by the sight of a jaw-dropping waterfall. And I've got to say, the journey doesn't stop there. We've got another hour ahead of us to reach Playas del Coco on the Pacific Ocean, with plenty of highway miles to let Dai-fat-zai flex his drifting skills like a pro.

Finding the entrance to Catarata Llanos de Cortes Waterfall was a breeze. As I pulled over to check out some street signs, a lively young boy pops up out of nowhere, offering up fresh green coconuts like it's nobody's business:

"Fresh green coconut, care for one?"

With his sun-kissed face and eager eyes, this kid's innocence is contagious. I couldn't resist – "Sure, make it three!" I shout back, grabbing some for my crew.

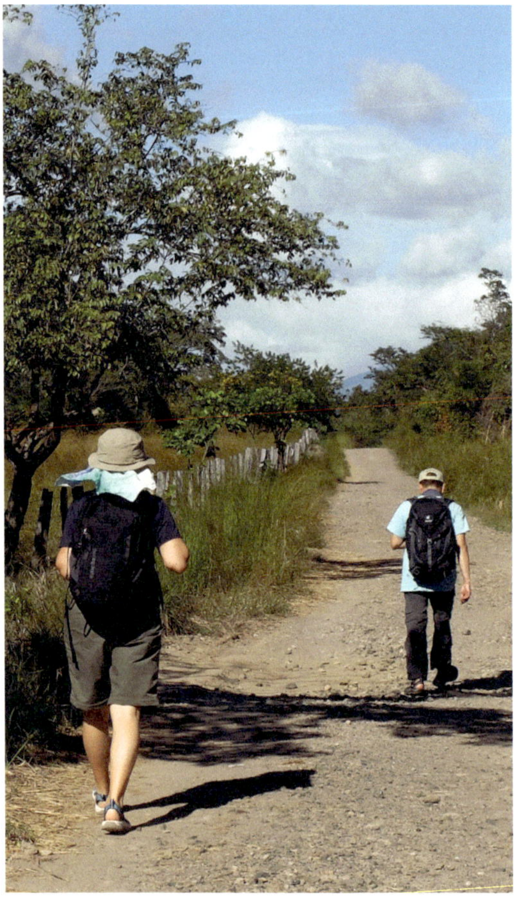

The kid practically skips back to his stall, shouting the good news to an elderly man nearby. In no time, he's back with the refreshingly cool coconuts, ready to fuel our adventure.

As I gaze up at the vast blue sky, the piercing rays of the sun catch me off guard. It's funny how time seems to slip away, making me realize it's December, nearly Christmas time. Back home, December is all about chilly rain, but here I am, leisurely sipping on a refreshing green coconut under the scorching midday sun. It's a scene straight out of a postcard, with kids from school taking a break to serve these coconut delights. I can't help but wonder if this little guy is enjoying his break or missing out on his school time for work.

After slurping down those delicious green coconuts, we followed the signs and checked out this waterfall everyone was raving about. The path there was no joke – just a gravel road stretching out into the distance.

Man, that sun was out to get us, no doubt about it. I had my trusty sun hat on, but it felt like I was walking through a sauna. And you know what? That water bottle? My lifeline. I must've chugged it down a hundred times, but it felt like I couldn't quench my thirst no matter what. Isn't it funny how drinking water can sometimes make you even more thirsty?

Thinking back on those refreshing green coconuts we had earlier, it's like they left me craving more than just a cold drink. Do you ever have those moments where something so good just leaves you wanting more? It's like chasing that feeling of pure bliss, hoping to capture it again and again.

Finally, after a short stroll, we catch our first glimpse of the waterfall. And this waterfall, instead of this towering giant you'd expect, it's like this sprawling wonder stretching out before us. People are already splashing around in the lake at the bottom, so of course, I couldn't resist diving right in.

As I immersed myself in the water, it was like a godsend after that sweltering walk. It washed away all the sweat and grime, leaving me feeling brand new.

So, there I am, paddling my way towards the waterfall, feeling the mist on my face as I get closer. I find this perfect little spot between the waterfall and the rock wall. And, oh man, the roar

Catarata Llanos de Cortes Waterfall

GPF2+QJ Bagaces, Guanacaste Province, Costa Rica

of that water was something else. It was like all the noise of the world just faded away, leaving nothing but me and the sheer power of nature.

And then, I did it – I climbed up to the rock and stepped right under that waterfall, with its thundering roar drowning out the world around me, I feel invincible. It's like nature's way of reminding me that sometimes, the best way to escape the chaos is to embrace it head-on. And the force of the water crashing down on me was like nothing I've ever felt before. It was like all my worries just washed away, leaving me feeling refreshed and alive.

After soaking it all in, I climbed back onto the rock, trying to catch a glimpse of the world beyond that curtain of water. But here's the thing, all I could see was white. And in that moment, it was like the outside world didn't even matter. All that mattered was me, that waterfall, and the feeling of pure bliss.

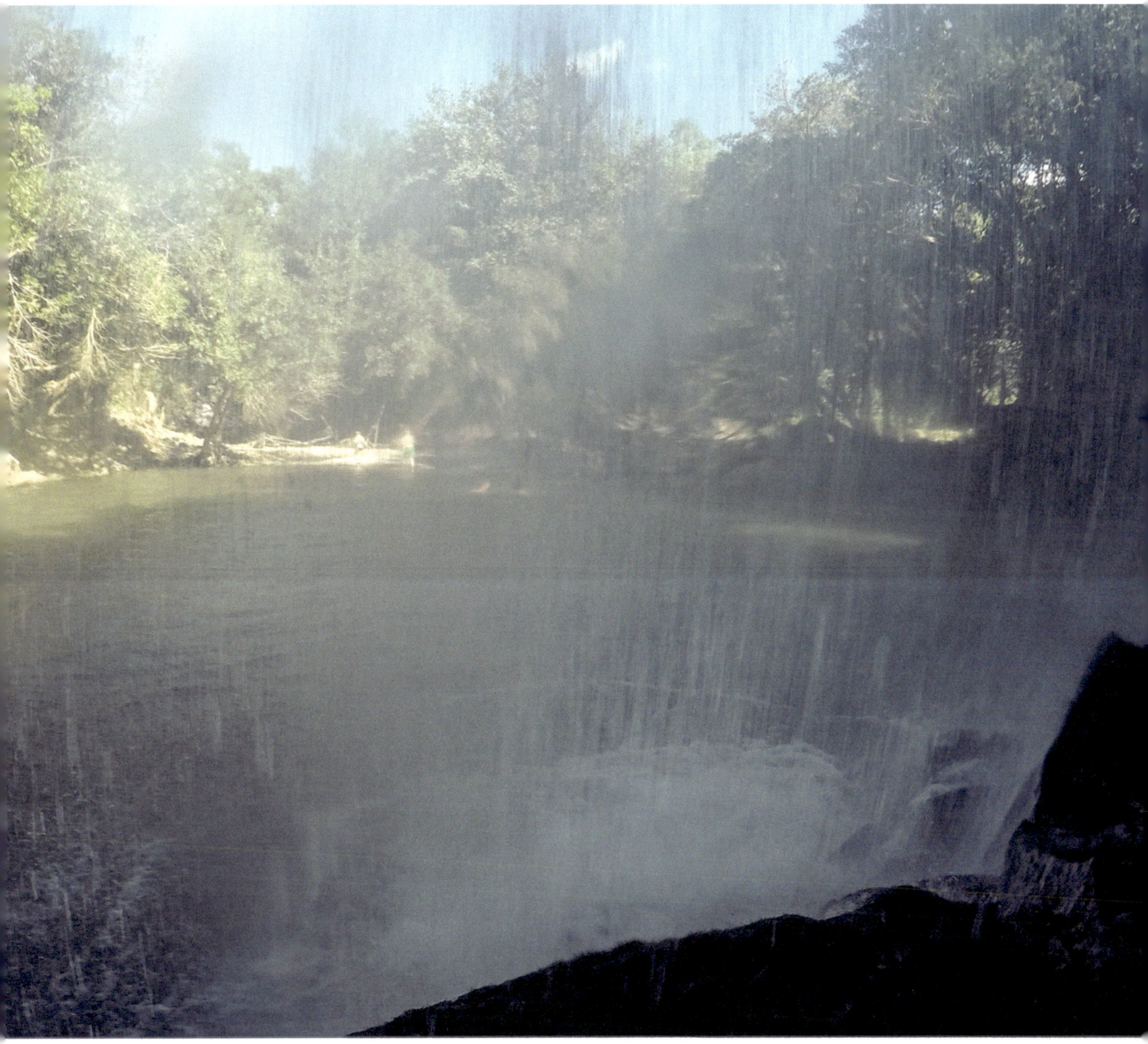

Llanos de Cortés

56 min / 63 km

Playas del Coco

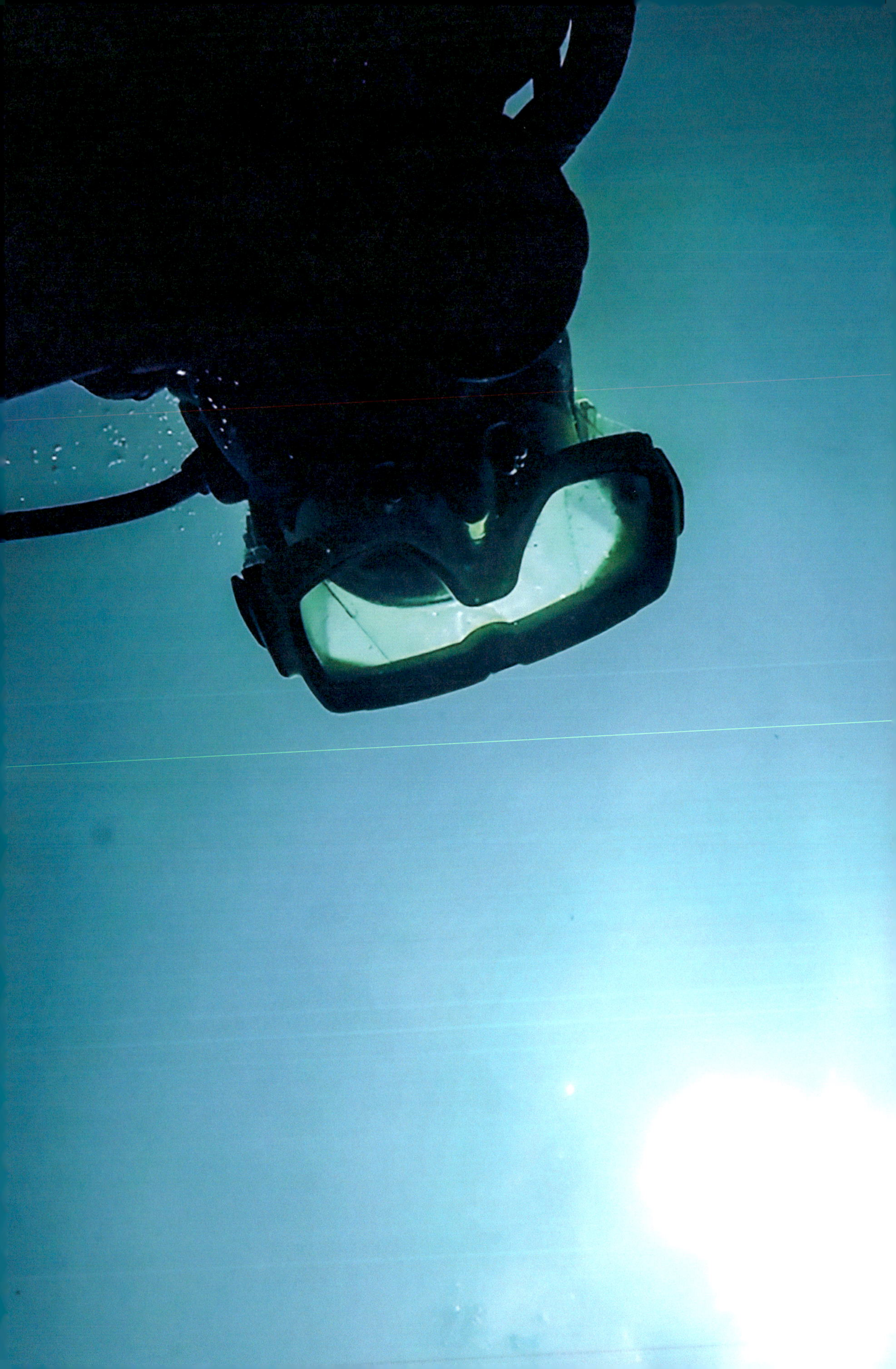

Diving without Depth: Secrets of the Deep

Leaving the majestic waterfall behind, hopping onto Dai-fat-zai, it's just a short hour's drive to the sun-kissed shores of Playas del Coco on the Pacific coast.

Now, don't get me wrong, Playas del Coco might not bag the title for the prettiest beach in Costa Rica, but I had my reasons for picking this spot. You see, it's a hotspot for diving enthusiasts like myself. Catalina Island boasts some of the best snorkeling spots with giant mantas, while Bat Island is teeming with bull sharks. If you're up for some face-to-face encounters with these magnificent creatures, this is the place to be. These dive sites are a bit of a jaunt, about 20 to 30 kilometers off the coast, with depths ranging from 75 to 100 feet and waves that can give you a good ride. Definitely not for the faint-hearted, but perfect for those who fancy a bit of an aquatic adventure.

Rolling into town around four in the afternoon, I wasted no time and made a beeline for the nearest diving shop. The enthusiastic young chap behind the counter gave me the lowdown on various dive sites, but my heart was set on Catalina Island. After checking out my diving credentials, he raised a brow and asked when was the last time I took a dive.

"Almost a year," I confessed, citing the cruel reality of limited vacation days.

With a knowing nod, he advised against Catalina due to its strong currents and suggested warming up with other sites first. Sensible advice, but alas, my time was short, bound back to La Fortuna the day after next.

"Perhaps next time," he suggested with a grin.

Heeding his wisdom, I swapped Catalina for another gem, Cabeza de Mono – Monkeys Head!

Bright and early the next day, the sun painted the beach with its warm hues as I strolled barefoot, feeling the cool sand beneath my toes. Joining the bustling crowd, I was taken aback by the sea of eager faces donned with diving gear. Turns out, they were all here for their diving certificates, adding to the excitement in the air.

After a brief wait, we hopped onto motorized sampans that whisked us to larger speedboats. In the midst of the commotion, I found myself on a smaller vessel with just four others. As we cut through the waves, I stood alone on the side of the speedboat, looking at the blue sky and green water. The strong wind brought the sea water and hit me in the face. Occasionally, when I encountered a wave, the boat jumped high like a frog and then hit the water, and the water splashed on me. It was a sensation of unrestrained freedom that I cherished each time I ventured out to sea for a boat dive.

Ten minutes later, we're on the boat, getting ready for an adventure-packed dive. Two divers are busy setting up their professional photography gear, suggesting we're in for some breathtaking underwater sights – perhaps coral gardens or majestic sea turtles. Can you feel the excitement bubbling up?

I double-check my gear, making sure those oxygen tanks are securely fastened and the regulators are good to go. Now, here's where things take a bit of a twist. Our young dive master, bless his soul, decides to play the strong silent type. No briefing, no pointers, nada.

Cue my puzzled expression. "Hey, what's the deal with this dive site?" I pipe up, expecting some pearls of wisdom.

And what do I get in response? A nonchalant "Don't worry, just jump when you're ready." Um, excuse me? That's it?

Now, I've been on a fair share of dives, I know the routine and this ain't the norm. Usually, the dive master fills you in on what to expect – the cool critters you might encounter, any safety tips. But not this time.

Luckily, one of my dive buddies swoops in for a gear check, and we give each other the thumbs-up. So, with a mix of nerves and excitement, I take the plunge. The chilly embrace of the sea welcomes me, and it's go time! Gear check one last time, and down I go into the depths, ready

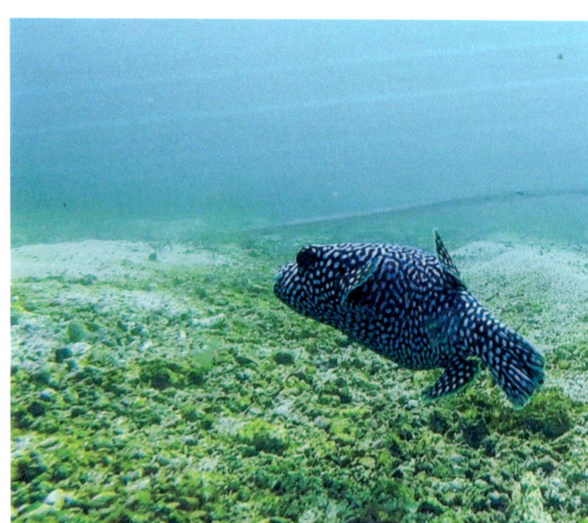

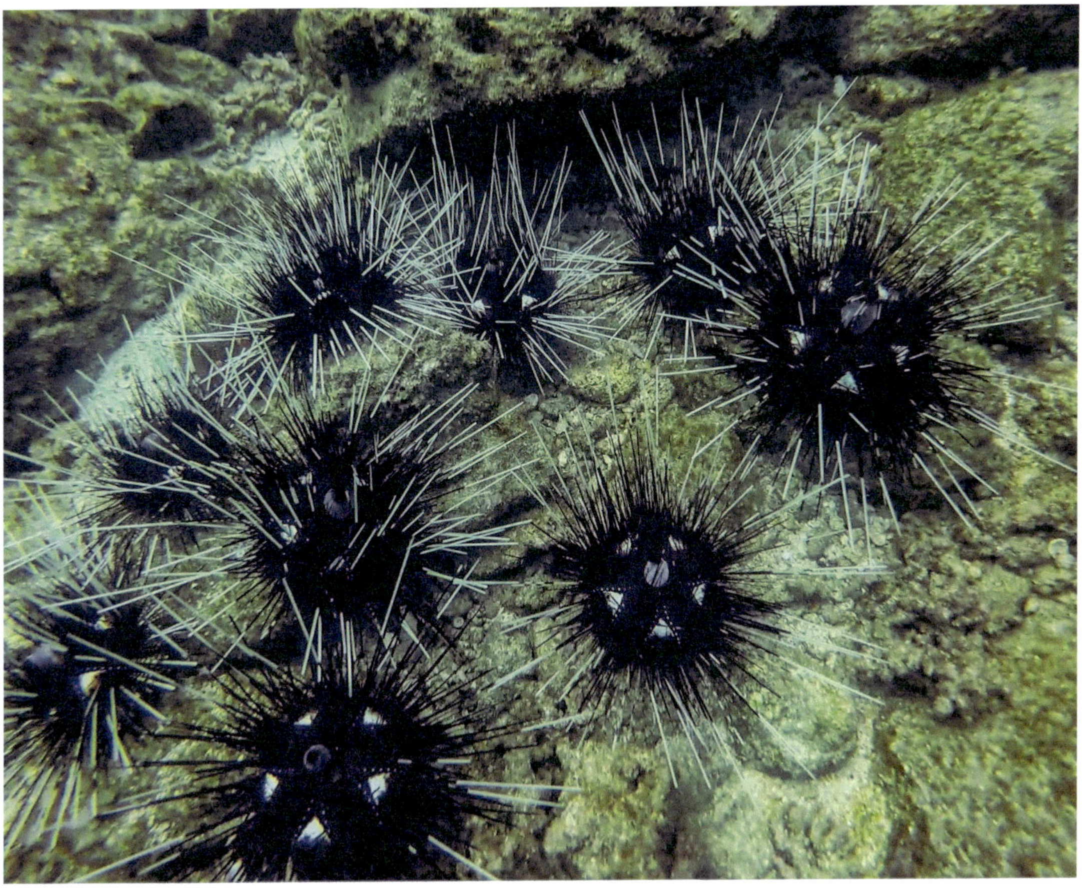

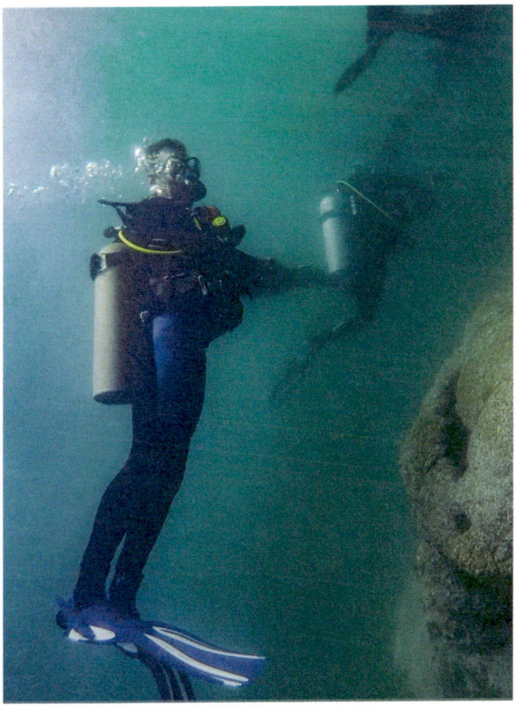

for whatever the underwater world has in store.

So there I was, cruising underwater, doing my thing. But as I hit about ten feet, my ears start doing that funky balancing act. No biggie, right? Just part of the dive routine. So, I soldier on, adjusting my buoyancy, checking my oxygen levels, the whole shebang.

But hold up. Something's off. I glance at my depth gauge and... wait, why does it insist I'm still chilling at ten feet? A quick reality check – bubbles rising, folks below me – yeah, I'm definitely deeper than that.

Panic's starting to trickle in, but I take a deep breath (literally, thanks to the regulator) and remind myself to keep cool. Life-supporting gear? Check. Broken depth gauge? Not ideal, but we'll roll with it.

I swim over to the dive master, waving my hands like a madman to signal my tech glitch. His response? A quick glance, a tap, a shake, and a casual "you're good." Not exactly the reassurance I was hoping for.

Now, normally, you'd expect a bit more support from the dive master, right? Like, maybe a signal to stick close in case things go south? But nah, not this guy.

So, with Plan A out the window, I switch to Plan B: stick close to the group, mentally rehearse those emergency drills, and try to shake off the jitters.

After a few heart-pounding minutes, the nerves settle, and I find my groove again, just floating along like it's no big deal. Because hey, in the unpredictable world of scuba diving, sometimes you gotta roll with the punches and trust in your own instincts.

Picture this underwater wonderland: a kaleidoscope of colors and creatures swirling beneath the surface. The water's this mesmerizing blend of light greens and blues, with moss-covered gray rocks adding a touch of rugged charm.

But hold onto your fins, 'cause it gets even better. Picture black sea urchins with spiky thorns, just chilling on the sandy floor, while chubby pufferfish dart between the rocks, flaunting their roundness like underwater beach balls. And then there's these long pipefish, gliding through the water with grace, like they own the place.

Oh, and let's not forget the locals – big-headed moray eels peeking out from their rocky hideouts, Panamanian sergeants schooling together, and teeny tiny seahorses striking a pose next to the rocks, looking all stoic and wise.

As if that's not enough, peeking up, you catch a glimpse of the dazzling blue sky, separated by the shimmering sea. With all this beauty, you'd bet your mask this spot's gotta be at least 75 feet deep. Ah, the magic of the ocean – always surprising, always enchanting.

You know, some folks reckon being underwater is all serene and tranquil, but as a scuba diver, I tell you, it's a whole different ball game. Every breath I took felt like it echoed through the depths, the sound of bubbles dancing around me as I exhaled. And don't even get me started on the noises – sometimes it's like the water itself is alive, with fish chattering away like they've got a lot to say.

It's like stepping into a whole other universe down there, where us humans are just visitors. Every dive feels like a mini adventure, a rollercoaster of floating and sinking, never quite knowing what you'll stumble upon next. And despite the lack of words or chatter, there's a strange kind of comfort in the solitude, a chance to soak in the magic of the underwater world all on your lonesome.

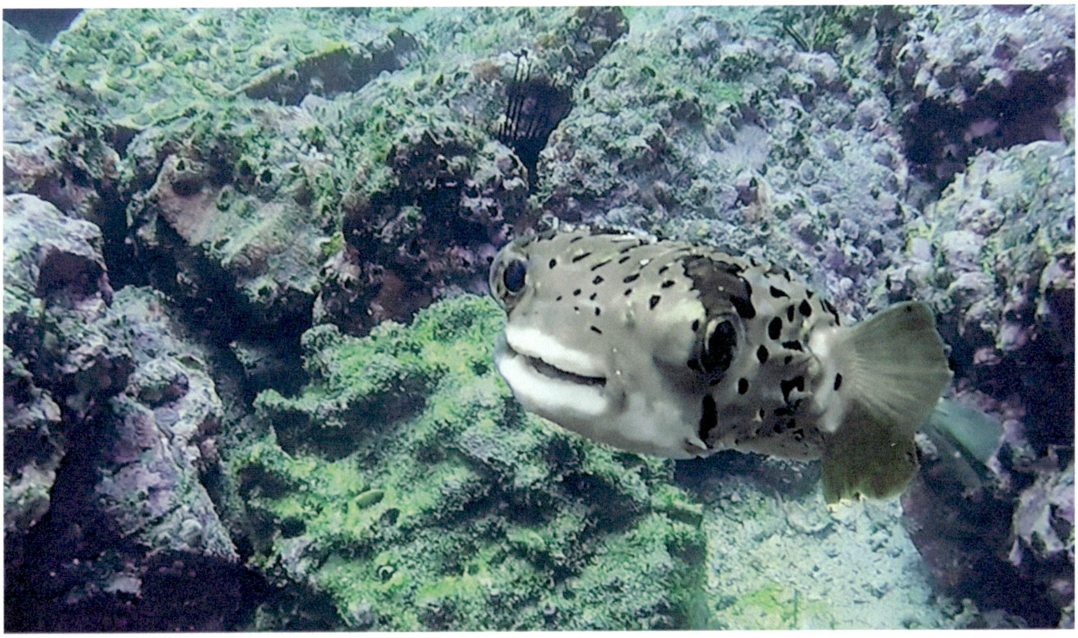

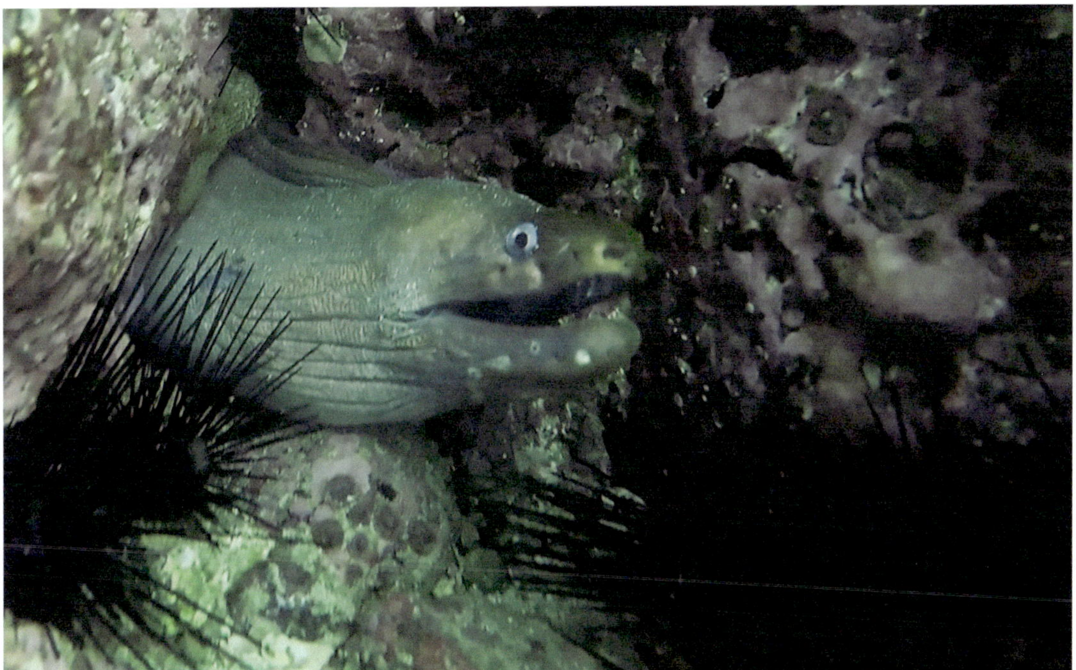

Playas del Coco

2 hr 58 min / 167 km

La Fortuna 1 hr 34 min / 97 km Los Chiles

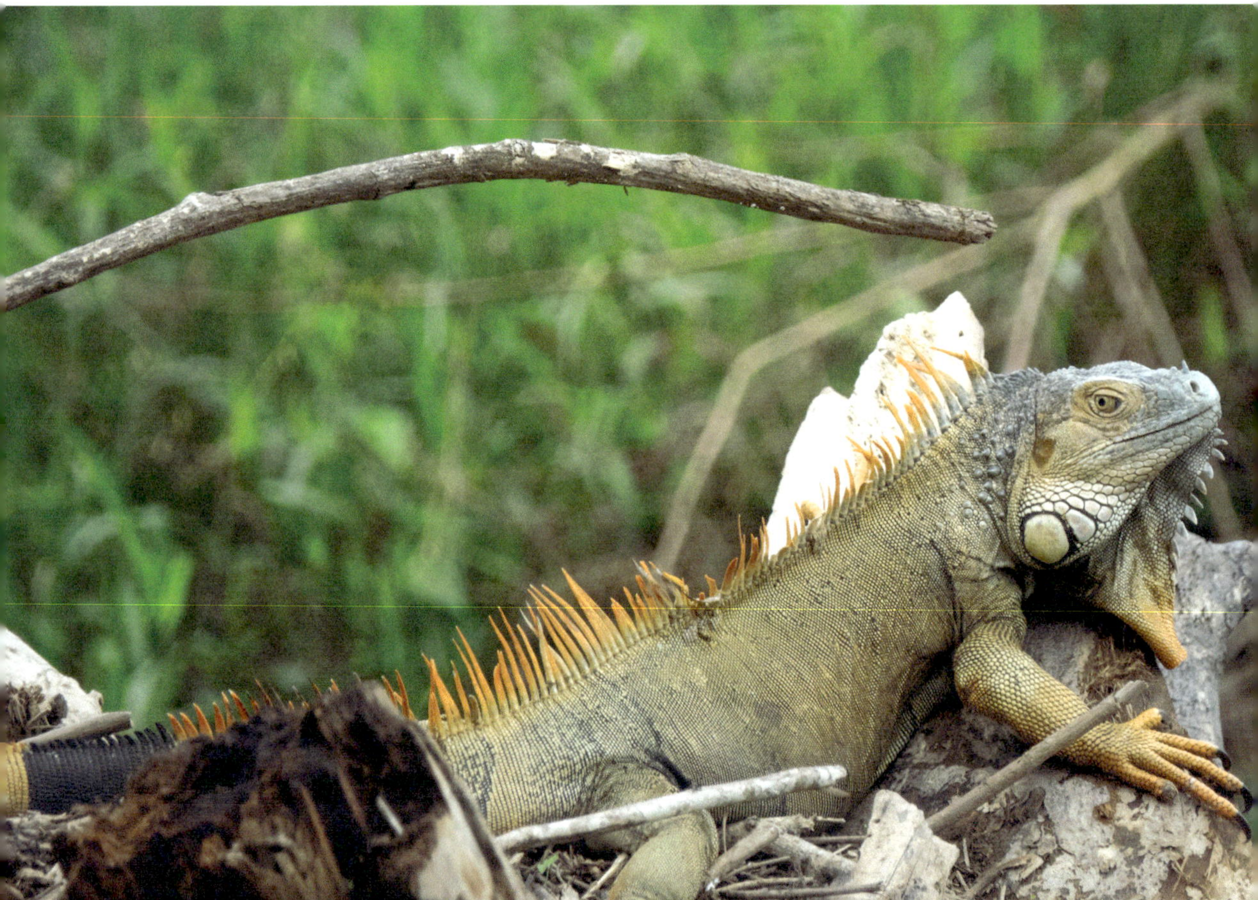

Transformative Journey: Life

As our journey wound down, we found ourselves back in La Fortuna after soaking up the sun in Playas del Coco. Our pit stop in La Fortuna was as simple and budget-friendly as it gets - a night in a cozy no-frills hotel and an early checkout the next day. But that was just the preamble to the real adventure awaiting us in Los Chiles.

Los Chiles, just a hop and a skip away from La Fortuna, set the stage for my next escapade. I jumped on board with a local tour group, all set for a riverboat ride through the Cano Negro Wetland National Wildlife Refuge. And boy, was I in for a treat! My camera went clickety-click capturing everything from crocs chilling in the sun to monkeys swinging from trees and even a parade of colorful iguanas.

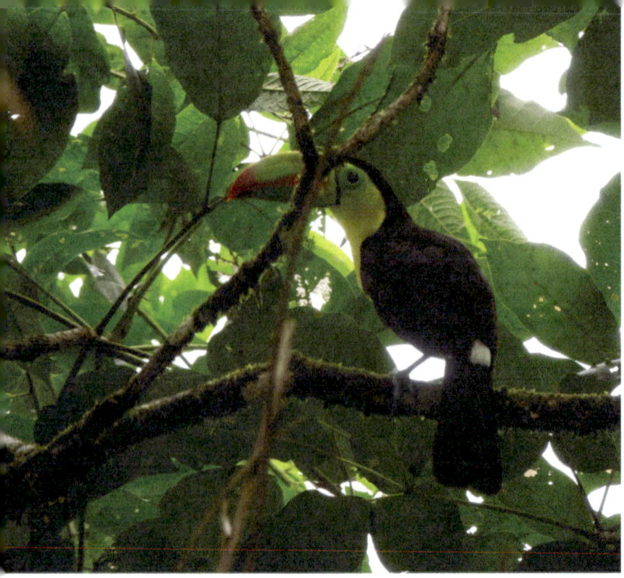

But the pièce de résistance? Spotting that elusive toucan I'd been daydreaming about. Its beak was like a painting, bursting with reds and greens, framed by those striking eyes and a splash of yellow on its neck. Trust me, no photo could do justice to its sheer beauty.

On our way back, we made a pit stop at a lone house in the middle of nowhere, where we were treated to a lunch that was as authentic as it gets. As we sipped on coffee, I found myself breaking out of my shell, chatting away with the friendly local family.

The old man, while setting the table, shared a little nugget of trivia with a grin plastered on his face: "This house? We built it ourselves. Saved a ton on wood by scavenging from an old dismantled house!"

"Wow, that's resourceful! Mind if I take a peek around?" I asked.

"Go ahead, make yourself at home!" he replied.

Stepping inside, I was greeted by an unexpected sight - a tiny Christmas tree and a chirpy little chicken. The geometric windows let in just the right amount of light, making the place feel warm and cozy. And the kitchen? A gas stove here, a wood stove there - I bet our lunch was whipped up on that wood stove!

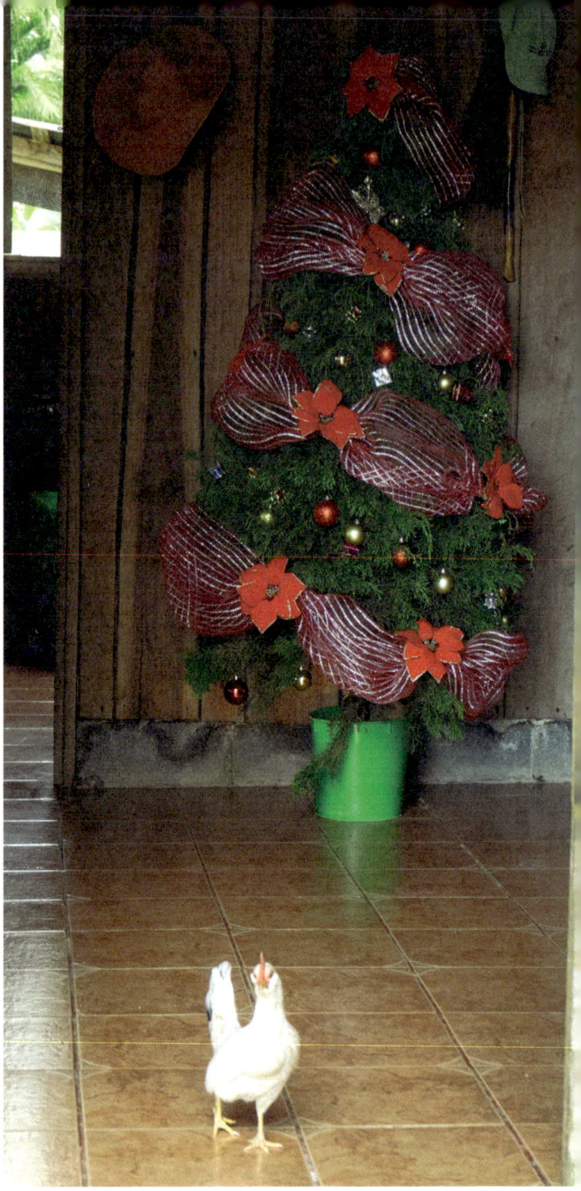

Back at the dining table in the front yard, I couldn't help but admire the simplicity of it all.

"Did you design those cool windows?" I asked, taking another sip of coffee.

The dad chuckled, "You bet! No need for fancy AC units around here. The night breeze works its magic, keeping things cool without inviting in any unwanted critters. And during the day, it's all about soaking up that natural sunlight - no need to flip on any switches!"

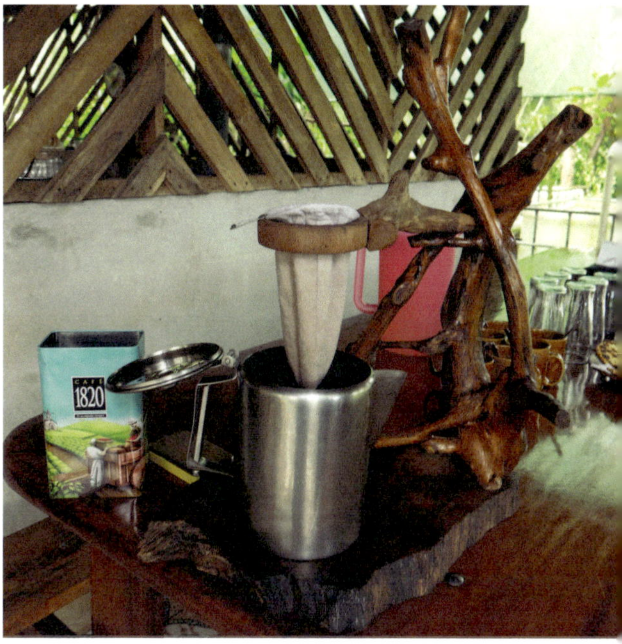

I was struck by his contentment with the simple life amidst the wilderness. "Why choose to live out here with so few comforts?" I prodded.

"Well, I've got a cozy roof over my head and a bunch of loved ones around me - what more could a person ask for, right? Used to be knee-deep in pineapple fields, sending those juicy fruits off to faraway places. But then, out of the blue, the importers decided our pineapples weren't up to snuff and slammed the door on us. Talk about a gut punch! So, I waved goodbye to the farming life, sold off the land, and put the dough into building this little oasis. Now, we're in cahoots with a travel agency, dishing out home-cooked lunches to wanderers like you and me. Sure, the cash flow ain't what it used to be, but hey, life's a whole lot simpler and sweeter now."

You know, I've always seen life as this hallway full of doors. When one closes, another swings open – it's like a constant game of chance. But what baffles me is how some folks cling to those closed doors, afraid to let go of what they know. Meanwhile, there's a whole world of opportunities right in front of them, just waiting to be explored.

And here's the thing: every closed door comes with a hidden gift. It might not be obvious at first, but there's always something positive waiting on the other side. The key is finding contentment in the hallway itself – because that's where the real magic happens.

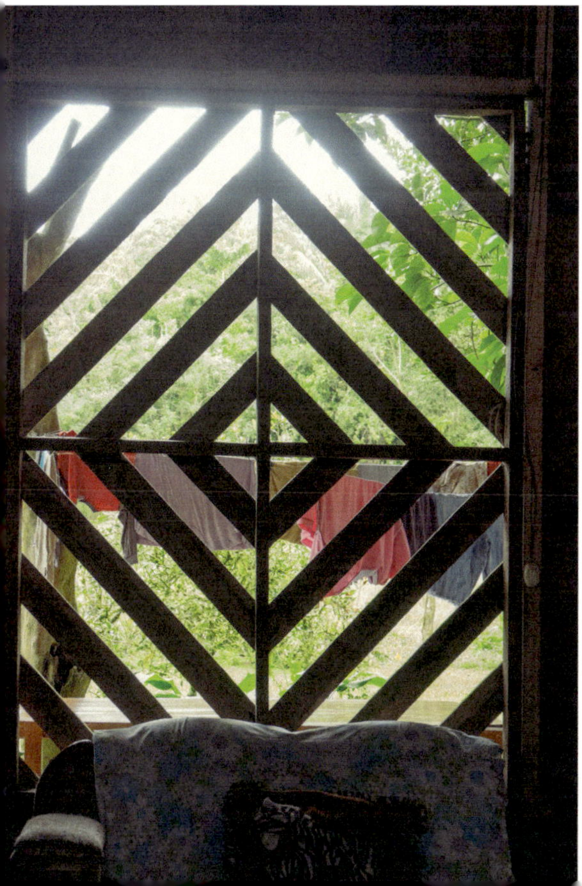

Caño Negro Wetlands National Wildlife Refuge

Caño Negro Los Chiles Alajuela, Provincia de Alajuela, Caño Negro, 21402, Costa Rica

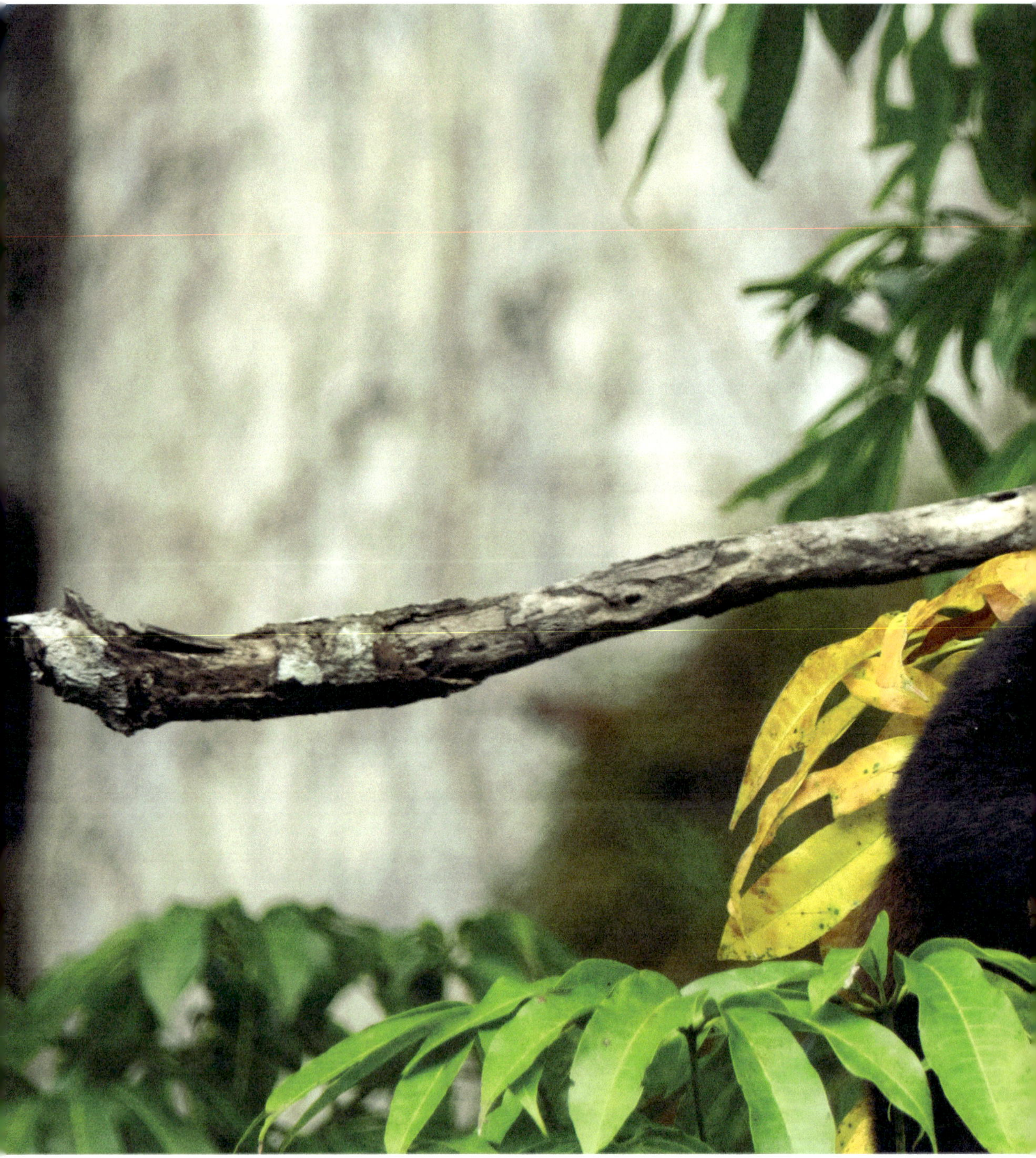

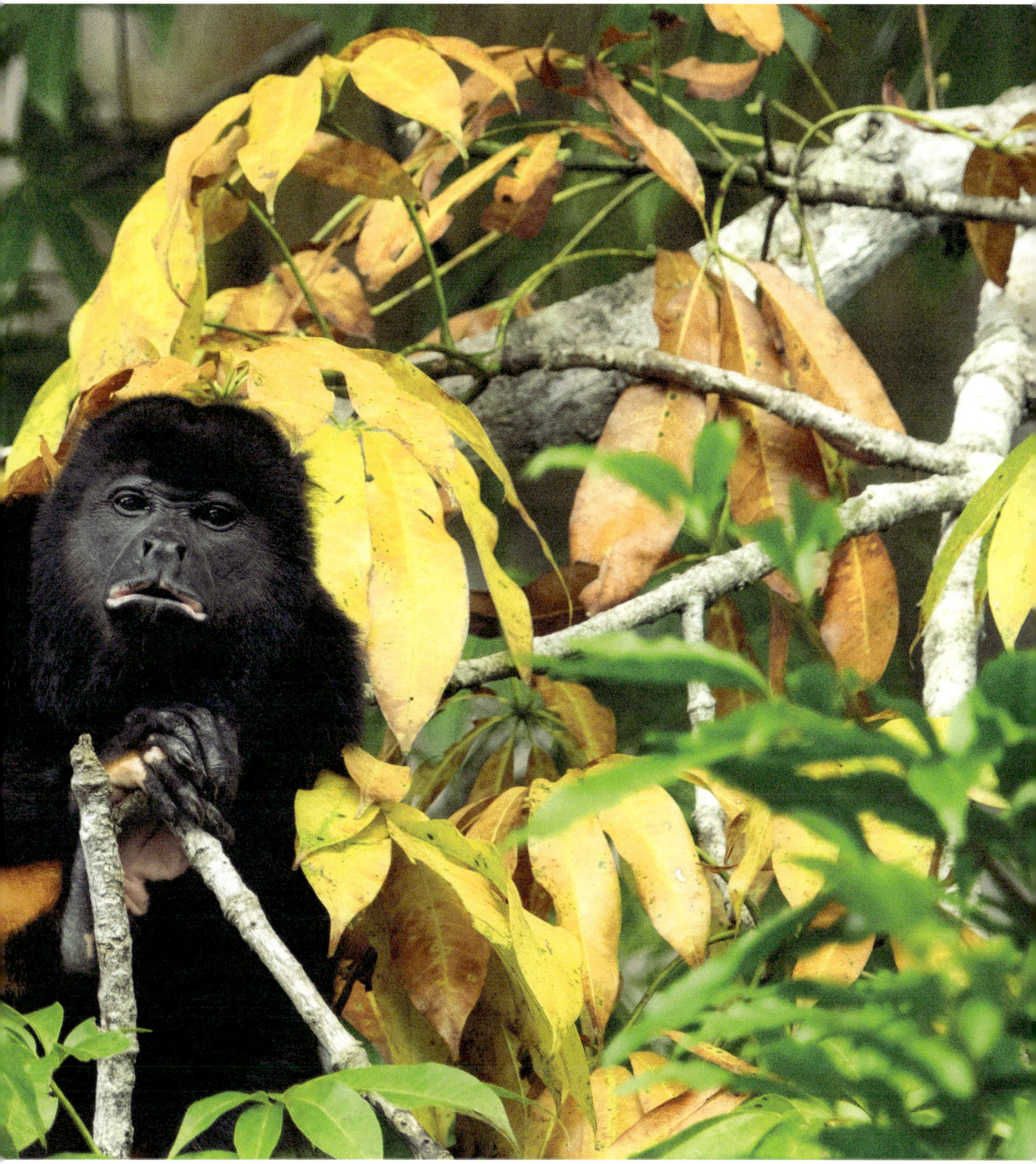

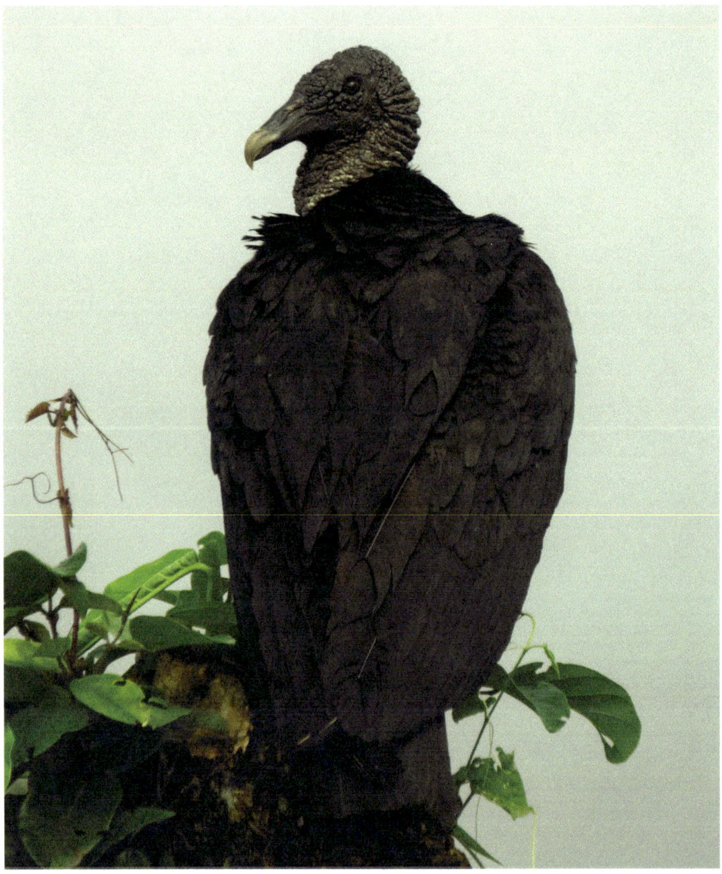

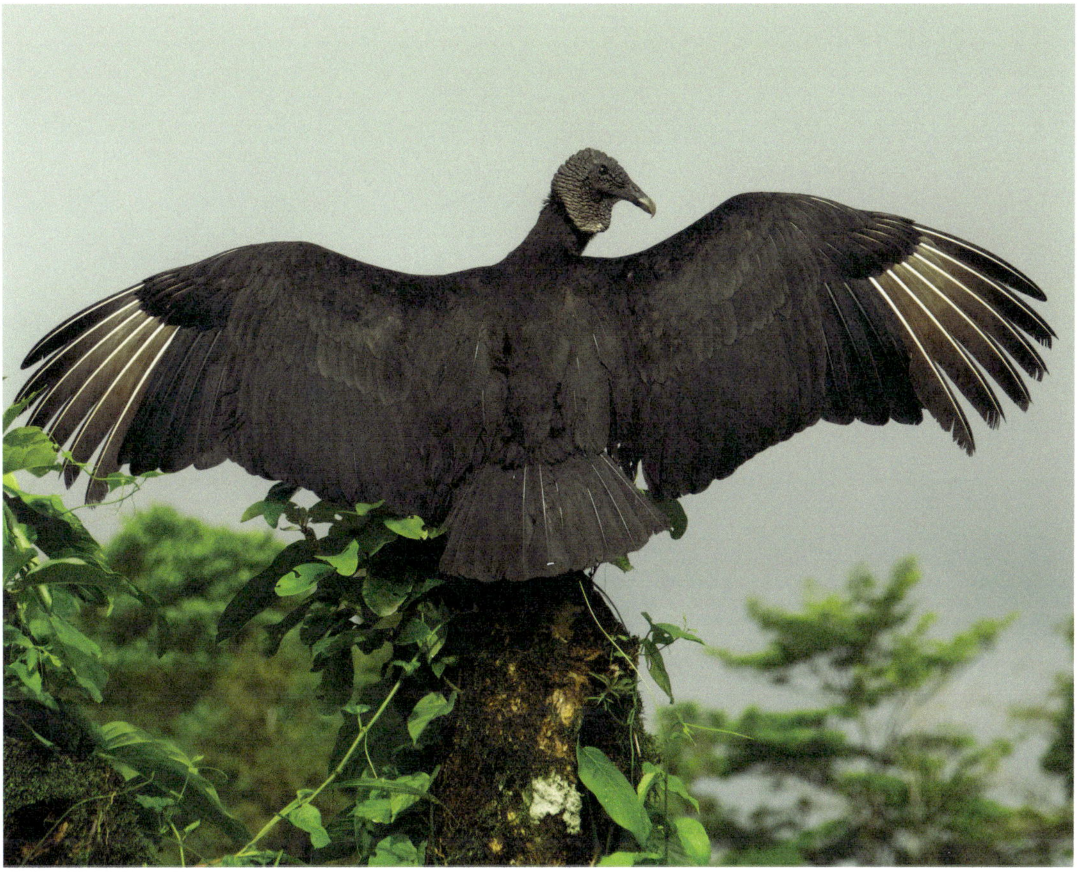

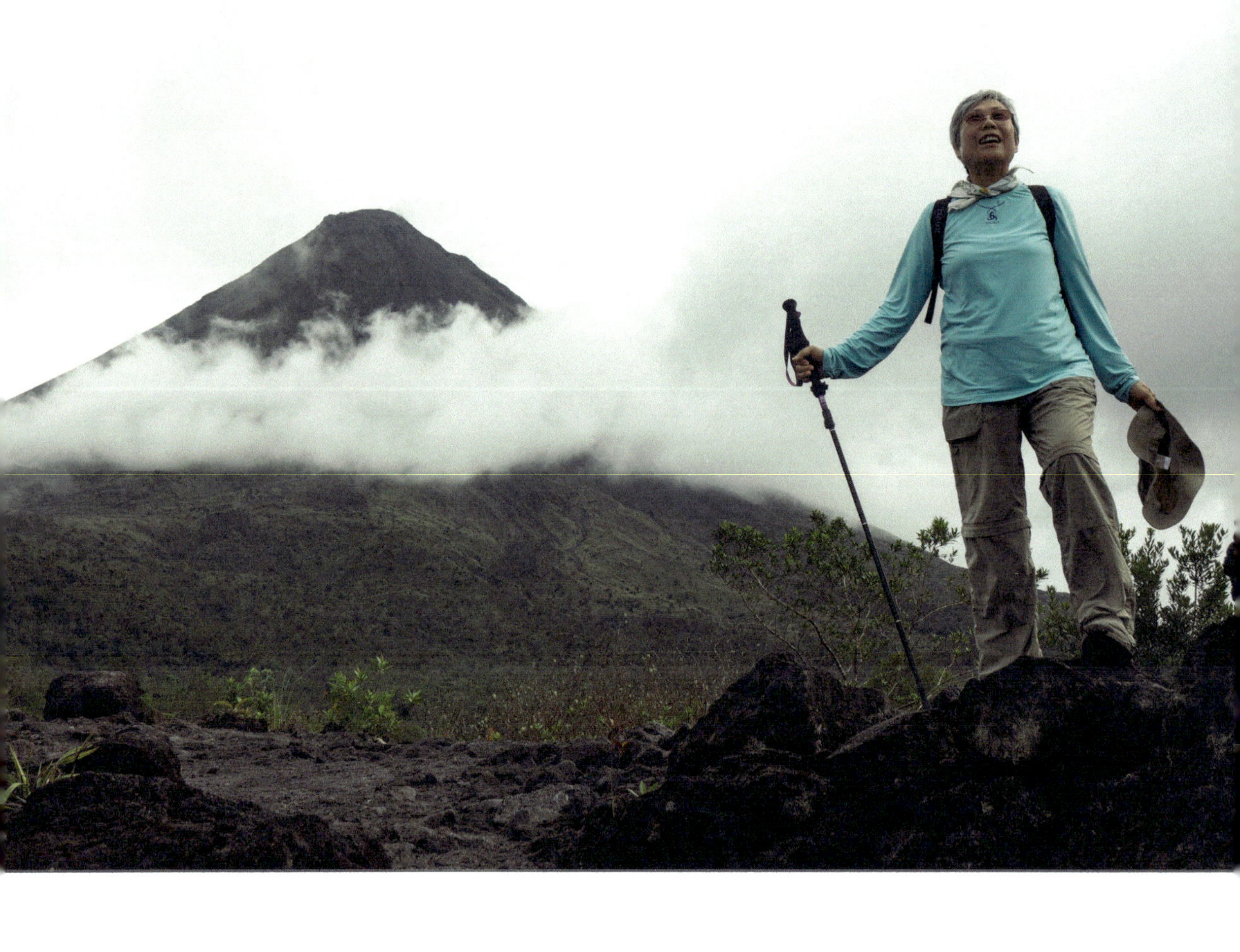

Traces of Flame

Back at the La Fortuna hot spring resort, I landed in a hotel boasting thermal springs - talk about a perfect recipe for relaxation! My plan for a three-day chill sesh got a wild twist when I woke up to a sunny day breaking through the clouds. Seizing the moment, I decided to hit up the Arenal 1968 Volcano View and Lava National Park. With a name like that, you know it's gonna be epic!

Named after a volcanic eruption that rocked the year '68, this park is a treasure trove of hiking trails snaking through lava-covered ruins. I opted for the longer mountain trail, hoping to get up close and personal with the volcano. So, off I went, zipping Dai-fat-zai up to the park entrance and sliding into a parking spot. Just as I was about to chill out, a staff member strolled over, motioning for me to crack open my window.

"Hey there! Can you reverse-park with the front facing the exit? It's just a little safety precaution in case things get wild," the staff member casually explained.

No biggie. I flicked the gear into reverse, swung Dai-fat-zai around, and snagged my tickets. It hit me then - we're dealing with an active volcano here, folks. Talk about playing it safe!

As I made my way up the mountain path, butterflies danced around like they owned the place. But the real MVPs? The mosquitoes. Those buggers were relentless! Thankfully, I had my trusty mosquito defense on standby. Along the way, I stumbled upon some cool magma rocks scattered amidst the lush greenery, reminding me that nature's a master of contrasts.

And then, just when I thought the hike couldn't get any cooler, I caught a glimpse of the Arenal volcano summit peeking through the clouds. It was like something out of a dream! Standing there, staring into the crater, I couldn't help but imagine the chaos of '68 when this bad boy went full-on Godzilla mode, spewing flames and wreaking havoc. But you know what? Now it's all about peace and quiet, with lava rocks scattered around like relics of a fiery past. Even though the volcano is currently taking a snooze, its history still gives me chills.

Lost in my thoughts, I glanced back up to see the clouds quickly shrouding the volcano again, a reminder that for now, the mighty volcano would remain in its slumber. And with that, I continued my trek, grateful for the chance to witness nature's raw power up close and personal.

Arenal Volcano View and Lava Trails

F787+G9 Tabacon, Alajuela Province, Costa Rica

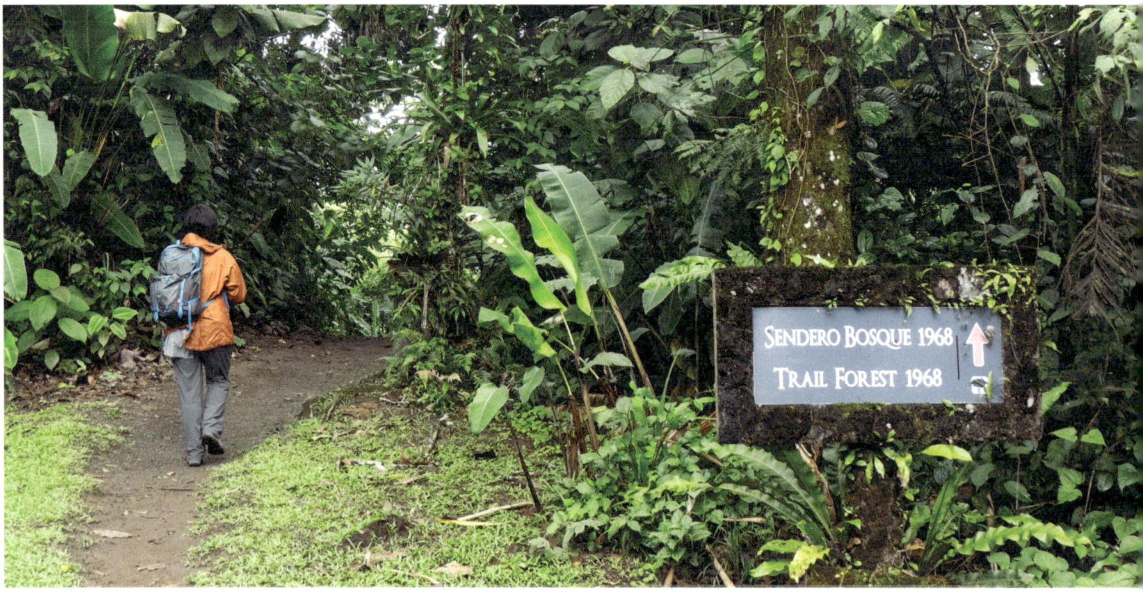

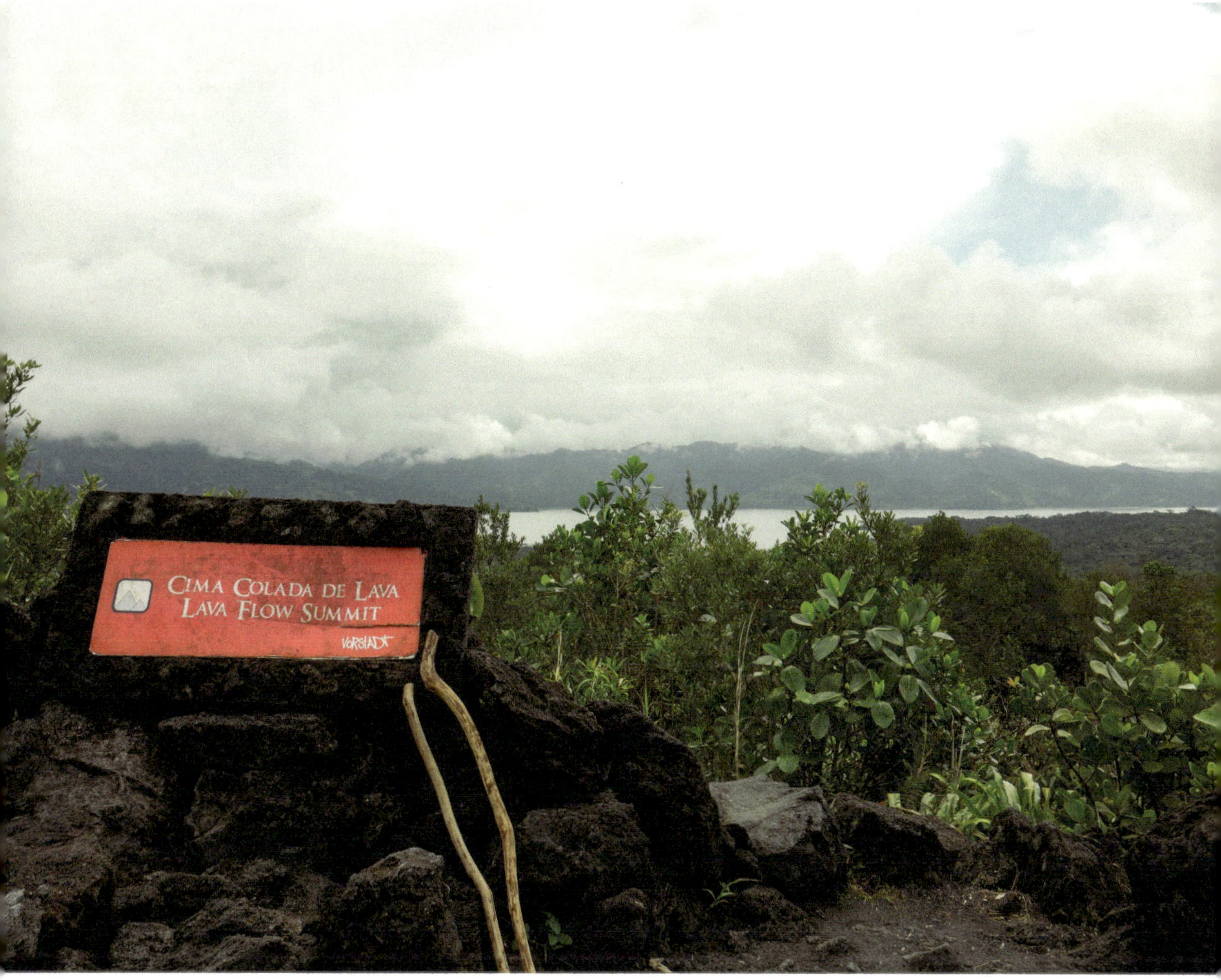
CIMA COLADA DE LAVA
LAVA FLOW SUMMIT

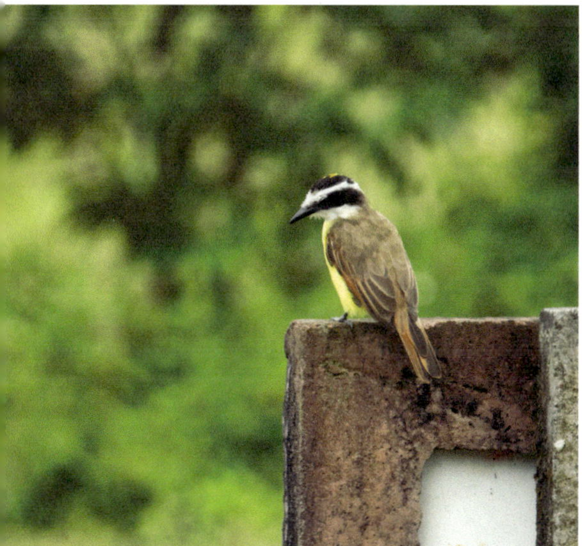

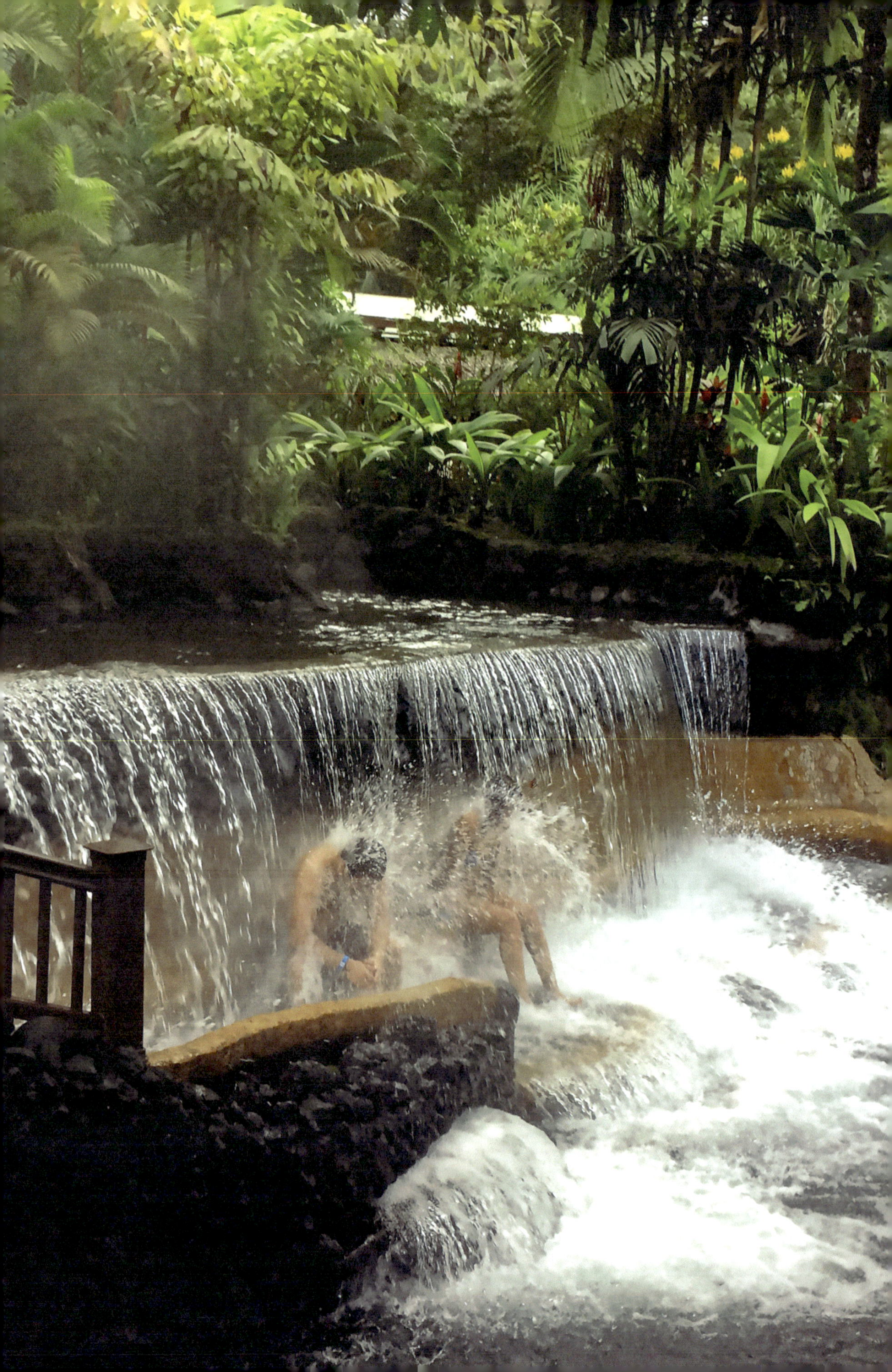

Farewell to Costa Rica's Freedom, Farewell to the Joyful Dai-fat-zai

So, after dancing in the rain, diving into calm lakes, chasing waterfalls, and even taking the plunge into the boundless expanse of the Pacific Ocean, here I am, wrapped in the warm embrace of natural hot springs. Tabacon Thermal Resort & Spa is like the hot spring jackpot, boasting over ten pools of all sizes, heated up by five different sources beneath the volcano. It's like soaking in nature's own Jacuzzi, with water trickling down from cascading waterfalls.

This hot spring adventure was a whole new ball game compared to my dips in Japan. Here, it's a mixed crowd, so you gotta gear up in swim trunks or swimsuits. Once I suited up, I jumped into one pool, switched to another every ten minutes, and kept up this merry-go-round routine. It felt less like a leisurely soak and more like a whirlwind tour!

Afraid of forgetting the colors of the world, leaving just to come back again!

In fact, I was really craving some solo soak time, so I decided to wait it out until the sun made its grand exit. No joke, it felt like discovering a hidden treasure - just a handful of people scattered across the pools, all lost in their own little worlds. So, after a bit of exploring, I stumbled upon this tucked-away hot spring, hidden from the hustle and bustle. It was like finding my own private oasis in the midst of it all.

The thermal water had this unique scent, almost like a hint of salty sea air. And as I lounged there under the starlit sky, with the gentle murmur of water in the background, I couldn't help but let my mind wander through every twist and turn of this unforgettable journey.

You know, every journey's got its own flavor, its own vibe. It's like wandering through museums in different cities - you pick up on similar threads, but each exhibit's got its own unique twist. And I gotta say, my trip to Costa Rica was no exception.

Here, it's a whole different story compared to the bustling subways and neon-lit streets. Instead of towering buildings and fancy museums, it's all about cruising along dirt roads in Dai-fat-zai, feeling every bump along the way. But you know what? There's something special about it - the freedom of exploring among the birds and animals, catching glimpses of misty volcanoes looming in the distance. And let's not forget the flavors! It's all about the simple pleasures here - hearty black beans and rich, aromatic coffee. Costa Rica's beauty is raw and unfiltered, and that's what makes it so uniquely captivating.

So, after saying our goodbyes to the hot spring haven, we hopped back into Dai-fat-zai and made our way back to San Jose. Dropping off the trusty ride at the car rental spot marked the end of our adventure. I'll tell you, those twelve days were something else.

Every single day was spent with Dai-fat-zai, and we really got to know each other. Despite not having all the fancy bells and whistles like a top-notch stereo or a super high-tech navigation system, Dai-fat-zai had something special. It was all about honesty and simplicity. Sure, it may not have been the fastest car on the road, but it was reliable, always pushing forward with a smile. Traveling with Dai-fat-zai brought back that sense of pure joy reminiscent of carefree childhood days.

As we concluded our journey, nostalgia flooded in, recalling the excitement of our first ride together and the anticipation of new adventures. I couldn't help but smile as I fondly remembered that moment when I excitedly exclaimed, 'Dai-fat-zai is back, let's go swimming!'

As I sat on the flight home, the lyrics of a song echoed in my mind: "Afraid of forgetting the colors of the world, leaving just to come back again!" It got me thinking, and I felt certain — I would be back.

Tabacon Thermal Resort & Spa

https://www.tabacon.com/

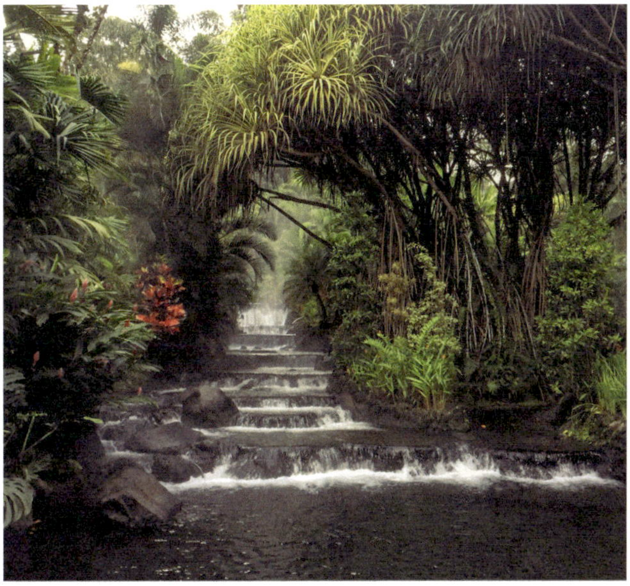

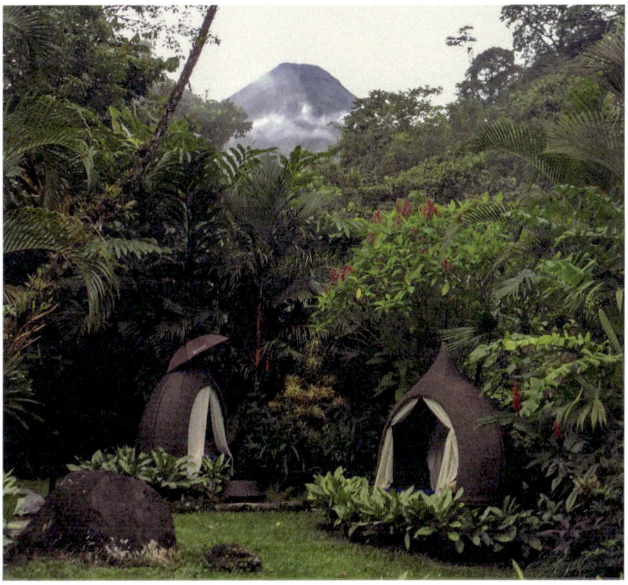

Cultural Mingle

Costa Rica:
Where Nature and Adventure Await!

Hey wanderers! Headed to Costa Rica? Pack your love for nature and wildlife because that's what makes this place tick. If you're into immersing yourself in local culture, consider volunteering. There are plenty of opportunities, especially in wildlife conservation. Sure, there is a cost, but think of it as an all-inclusive adventure package—food, accommodation, and hanging out with amazing critters. Sweet deal, right? Here's some info to help plan your trip.

Sea Turtle Conservation - *Location: Ostional Beach, Nicoya Peninsula (Pacific Coast)*
No matter which volunteer gig you pick, witnessing thousands of olive ridley sea turtles hitting the beach to nest is mind-blowing. Between July and November, you'll catch over 300,000 of them nesting during each arribada. Seriously, it's a sight you won't forget!

Rescue Center Assistant - *Location: Alajuela, Costa Rica*
Love animals? This program offers an awesome experience and the rewarding feeling of helping injured wildlife get back on track. You'll stay busy every day preparing food for over 100 animals and doing some cleaning and maintenance of their enclosures. It might sound tiring, but you'll be working with like-minded volunteers from all over the world!

Save our Oceans! - *Location: Garabito, Costa Rica*
This world isn't just for us; we share our land and oceans with animals and marine life. Unfortunately, we often mess up the ocean with plastic bottles, bags, and other trash. It's time to clean things up a bit. Sure, it might seem like dirty work, but hey, nobody wants to swim in a sea full of garbage, and our marine friends deserve better too!

One Night Homestay - *Proyecto Asis Wild Rescue Center, Garabito, Costa Rica*
This program is more than just volunteering—it's an adventure! You'll explore the Proyecto Asis Wildlife Rescue Center, stay with a friendly host family, help care for animals, and enjoy a fun sloth tour. Plus, you'll get to savor a delicious Costa Rican dinner and experience a cultural exchange. It's an unforgettable experience!

Environmental Research and Education - *Location: Tortuguero, Costa Rica*
In this project, you'll explore a protected area with incredible wildlife. You'll compost, care for nurseries, clear trails, monitor animals, sift sand for plastic, teach kids, label turtle nests, reforest, help with dog spay/neuter days, patrol sea turtles, and monitor jaguars. It's a fun, hands-on way to make a difference and experience Costa Rica's beauty!

Disclaimer: The information provided herein is for informational purposes only. We do not guarantee its accuracy or completeness. Use at your own risk; we are not liable for any errors or any losses, injuries, or damages arising from its display or use.

Hello Hello

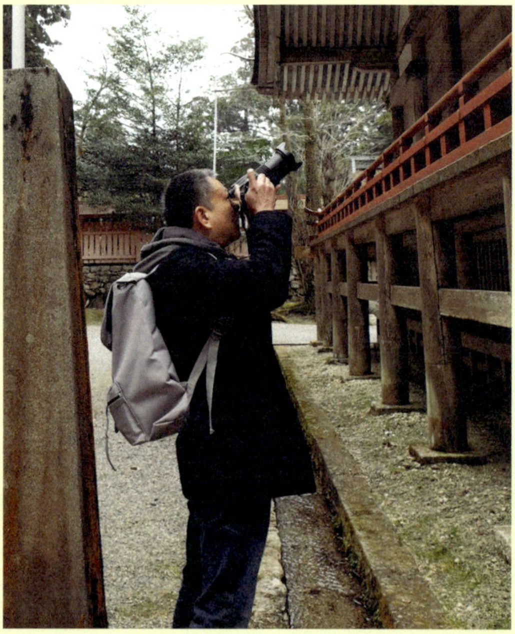

www.instagram.com/wing.can.fly

My name is:
Terence Lui

Q: Where are you based now? Are you always on the road, writing up a storm?

A: I currently call San Francisco home, but Hong Kong is where I originally hail from. By day, I'm a graphic designer, part of the weekday grind. But every 18 months or so, I hit the road for an epic adventure, breaking free from city life and recharging my creativity! Writing's my side gig—I've got a wild imagination, and spinning tales keeps me entertained and my creativity flowing!

Q: Is writing a travelogue a tough gig?

A: Writing, like any creative endeavor, has its ups and downs. When it comes to travel writing, you've got to capture the vibe of each place you visit and remember all the interesting chats you had along the way. It's all part of the craft. Oh, and fun fact—this travelogue is my first published book, and it was originally written in Traditional Chinese characters!

Q: What's your all-time favorite city and country?

A: No favorites or least favorites here! Just places I'll skip. If a regime is trampling on people's rights and freedoms, count me out. It's not about being scared of them; it's about not giving them a dime to fuel their nonsense!

Q: Who's your go-to travel guru?

A: It's gotta be Anthony Bourdain, right? This New York chef didn't just whip up amazing dishes; he also picked up a pen and wrote some incredible books. His stories dive deep into the lives of famous chefs and the gritty, intense world of professional kitchens. But then, he switched gears and became a travel show host.

On his show, Bourdain never just scratched the surface. He shared his unique perspectives and thoughts about every place he visited. At each city's dining table, he didn't just talk about whether the food was good or bad. Instead, he explored how food brings people together—chefs, waiters, market vendors—and through their stories, he delved into local culture and society. Sometimes, his insights even raised big questions about the world at large.

Bourdain's show wasn't just about eating, drinking, and having fun. It also tackled serious issues about society and the world, often leaving viewers with a mix of wonder, helplessness, and a touch of sadness—perhaps reflecting his own worldview. In the end, when he left us, he left behind a vibrant, colorful journey that was as thought-provoking as it was bittersweet.

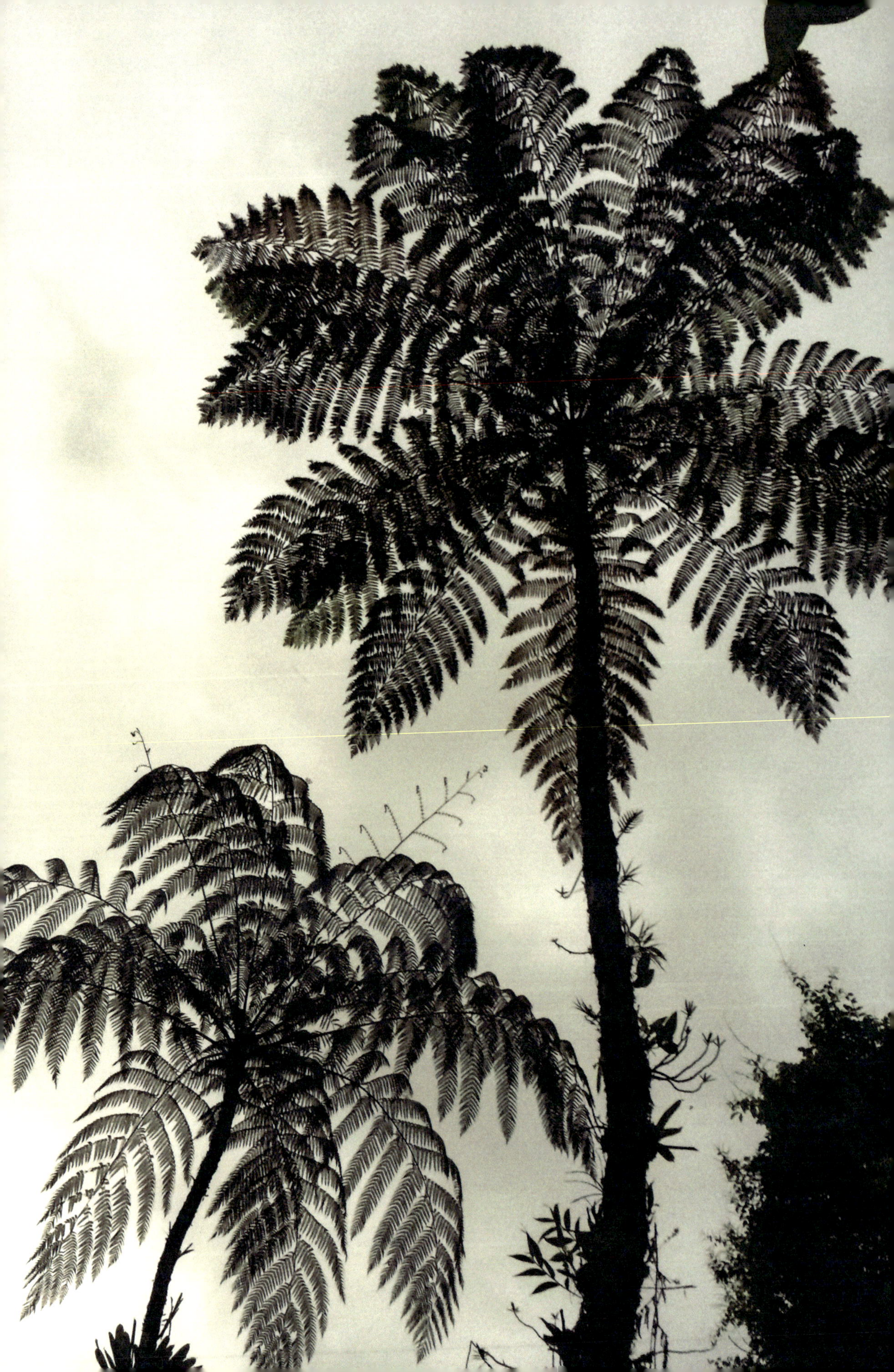

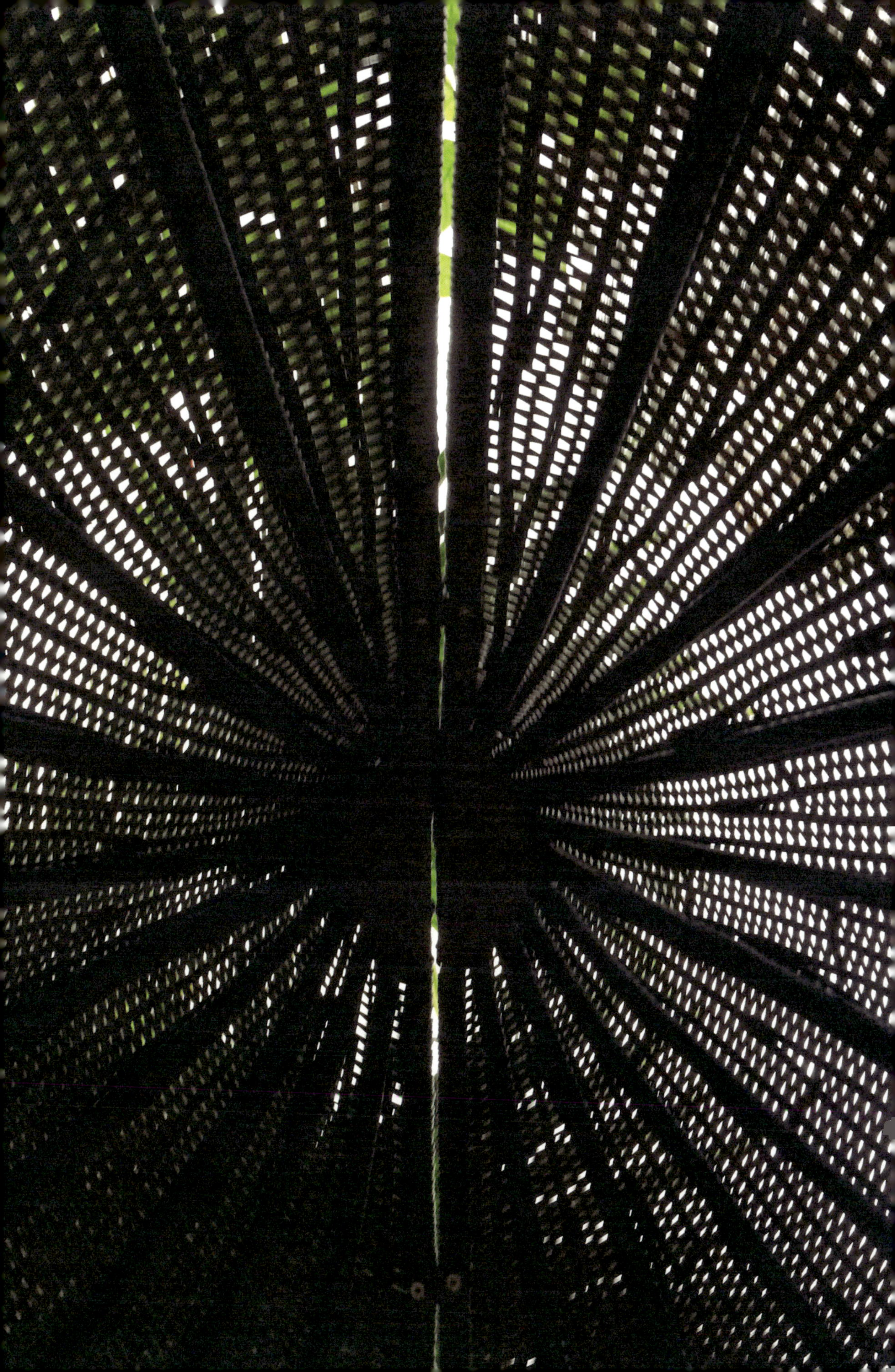

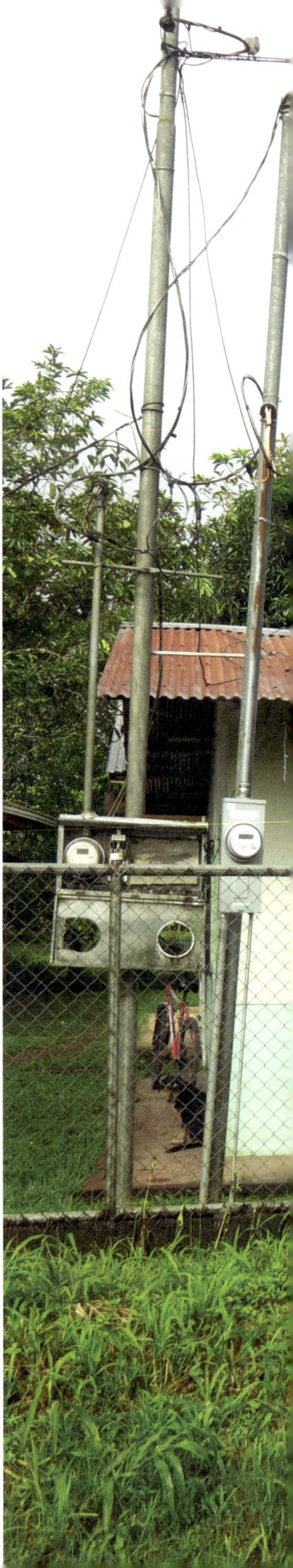

wingcanfly
Costa Rica: Unleash Freedom in the Wilderness

This book owes its existence to the invaluable support of my friends and family. Special thanks to Martina Ng, Tasia Laksmi, Derek Lui, Anne Guaspari and Sandy Ng.

Published by Belightful Living LLC

Text, graphic design, illustrations, and infographics by Terence Lui.
The original text was written in Traditional Chinese characters and translated into English by Google Translate and edited by ChatGPT.

First edition – Nov. 2024
ISBN 979-8-9911773-0-6

www.wingcanfly.com

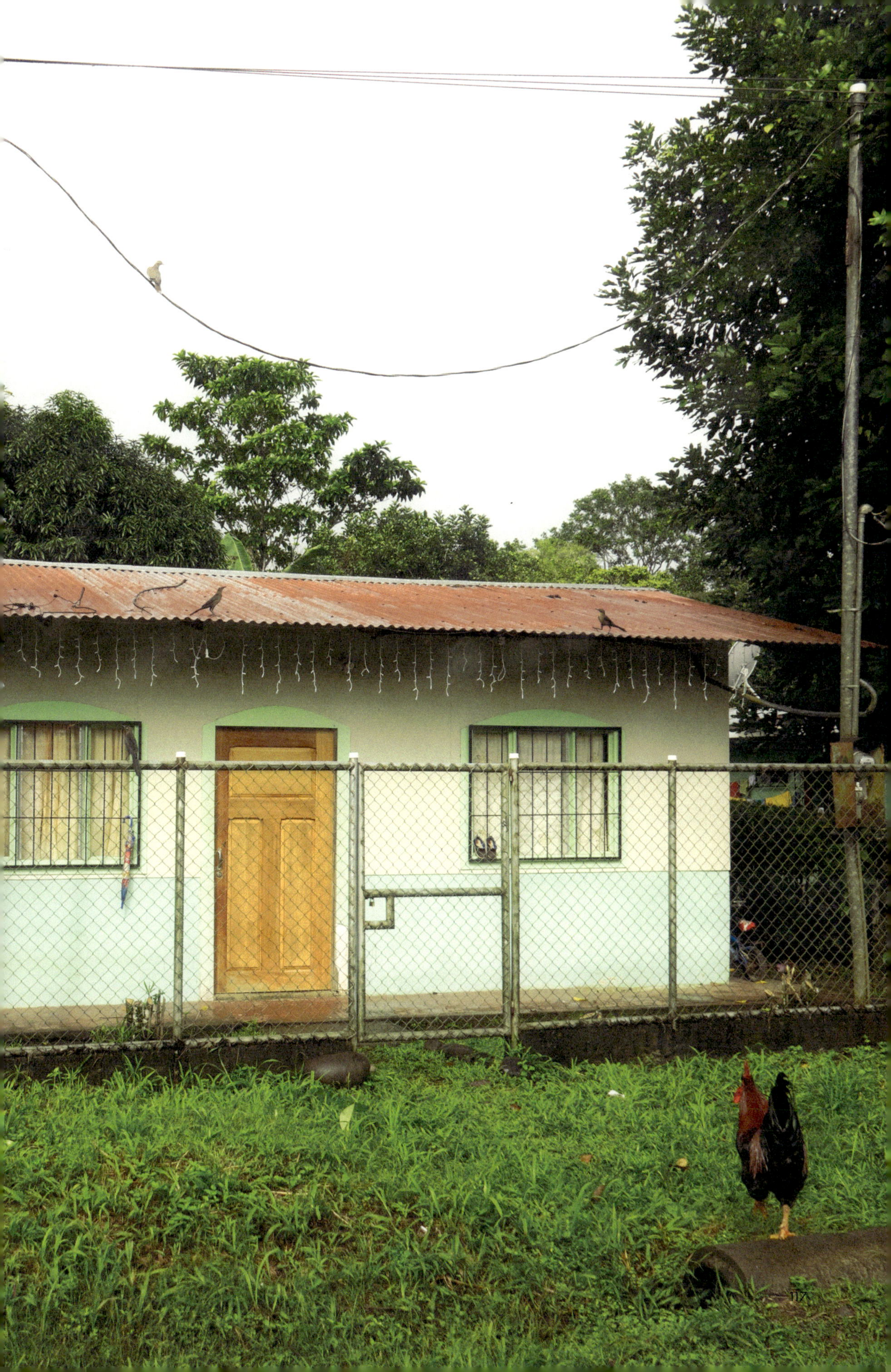

Made in the USA
Columbia, SC
05 January 2025

751221c1-d8e5-4273-b7b4-f875ba2616ceR01